TestWise

Strategies for Success in Taking Tests

Rona F. Flippo

Fitchburg State College
Fitchburg, Massachusetts

David S. Lake Publishers
Belmont, California

Dedication

To my children Todd and Tara Flippo, and to my parents Molly and Ted Fleig, for their love, support, and help throughout the years.

Special Acknowledgment

To Al Raygor, Professor Emeritus of Educational Psychology, University of Minnesota, my collaborator, with special thanks and recognition for his help and thoughtful comments throughout the development of this material.

ISBN 0-8224-6939-1

Printed in the United States of America
1. 9 8 7 6 5 4 3 2 1

Contents

Introduction

This book has a single purpose: to help you do the best you possibly can on every test you take. This is not a book on study skills in general; it is a book about one specific skill: test-taking. This is a book about how to be testwise.

To get the best score possible on a test, it is not enough just to know your subject thoroughly, although that is obviously necessary. You must also know how to prepare for and how to take essay tests and objective tests. The reason is that a test not only samples your knowledge of a subject, but it also measures your ability to take tests.

To get the best score possible on a test, it is not enough just to go to class, listen to the lectures, and do the assignments. You must also be able to demonstrate to the instructor that you know the content of the course so he or she can evaluate you and give you a grade. The more that you can demonstrate that you know, the higher your grade is likely to be. That is the way the system operates.

By being testwise, you can make the system work for you. Even if you are not the best student in the class, you will be better prepared and feel more confident if you know how to study for and take tests. Being testwise is not a gimmick; it means you have the essential skills to be a better student. The more you know about preparing for and taking tests, the higher your test scores are likely to be. That is what being testwise is all about.

What Is Being Testwise?

Being testwise is knowing how to play the testing game and come out a winner. It means that you know how to

1. get in the right frame of mind to take a test,
2. use all available resources to study effectively for both objective and essay tests,
3. anticipate the right questions for each test,
4. practice answering those questions before the test,
5. recognize the cues given in the test, and
6. use strategy to correctly answer as many questions as possible in the time allotted for the test.

How to Use This Book

This is an easy book to use because it guides you step-by-step toward becoming testwise, from the first day of the school term right through test day. Along the way, *TestWise* provides plenty of opportunities to practice using the tools and techniques that will help you get better test scores.

This book divides the process of becoming testwise into three parts:

- first, how to get yourself organized and in the right frame of mind to take tests,
- then, how to study for essay and objective tests, and
- finally, how to take essay and objective tests.

Some of the chapters present general testwise skills, and others present specific techniques for essay or objective tests. So there are two ways you can use this book: Work through it chapter by chapter to learn all the testwise skills, or work through only the general chapters and those that apply to the kind of test you are facing right now.

No matter what kind of test you will be taking, you should read Part One. Chapter 1 tells you how to avoid test panic. It provides advice and techniques for psyching yourself up, relaxing before and during tests, and making your course notes and readings useful study resources. In Chapter 2, you will learn how to plan for your tests each term. It shows you how to make a master schedule for all your tests, how to anticipate what each test will contain, and how to schedule your study time for them.

Part Two is about studying for tests. In Chapter 3, there are general test-study techniques. You will learn how to make study notes and how to memorize them, and you will learn the right way to cram before a test. Chapter 4 is about studying for essay tests—predicting various kinds of essay questions and practicing answers to them. Chapter 5 covers study techniques for the various kinds of objective questions: multiple-choice, matching, true-false, and completion.

Part Three is where you will learn how to take tests. Chapter 6 contains advice for getting ready on exam day so you can focus all your energy on doing well on the test. In Chapter 7 you will learn how to budget your time to take an essay test and how to write essay answers that are complete, clear, and to the point. Taking objective tests is the subject of Chapter 8. There, you 'll learn how to pace yourself so you'll have time to come back to questions that stumped you the first time around. And you'll learn the cues to look for in multiple-choice, matching, true-false, and completion questions to help you identify the right answers.

If you're facing an essay test, you can skip Chapters 5 and 8. If you're about to take an objective test, Chapters 4 and 7 won't be necessary right now. But to become completely testwise, you should work through the entire book. And after you've gone all the way through *TestWise*, you should keep it as a reference and return to the parts of it—relaxation techniques or the cues for multiple-choice questions, for example—that will help you prepare for future tests. So that you can stay testwise, blank copies of the test-study tools—study schedules and the test analysis form— are provided in the Appendix. Copy them and use them!

One last word about *TestWise:* This book is designed especially for teacher-made and departmental tests. Although much of the information here will help you with standardized tests, it is recommended that you also refer to the study manual for the particular test you are planning to take. Special study guides for the GED, SAT, ACT, CLEP, GRE, and other standardized tests are available from bookstores and libraries.

But no matter what kind of test you are facing right now, you owe it to yourself to become testwise about both essay and objective tests, and this book contains the most useful and accurate information to help you do that.

Part One

Getting Started

Chapter 1

Avoiding Test Panic

Tests measure students' knowledge of a subject or their ability to perform a skill. Tests are a means for students to show their instructors that they have mastered the course content, and they are a basis for instructors to assign grades. Granted, some tests are better or fairer than others, but, like it or not, the grades that are based on those tests are the measure of your success in school. Grades can determine if you will get a degree, if you will get into an advanced program, and even if you will get the job that you want.

Because tests can have all these consequences, it is quite understandable that all students at one time or another will be anxious about tests. A certain amount of anxiety is normal—and even desirable—because it motivates you to try to do your best. Just as runners get themselves psyched up before a race, actors before a performance on stage, football players before a game, lawyers before a trial, and business executives before a meeting with important clients, so students need to get themselves psyched up before a big test.

Too much anxiety, however, can spoil your performance. If you are too tense and too worried about doing well on a test, you will find it almost impossible to concentrate. When you try to read your class notes, the words seem like a meaningless blur, and when you sit down to take the test, your mind goes blank. These are the signs of too much anxiety.

In this chapter, you will find out how to be ready for a test without being panicked about it. You will learn how to psych yourself up for a test so you will *be motivated to do your best*, and you will learn how to relax and how to organize the course content so you will *be able to do your best*. These are the first steps to becoming testwise.

Psyching Up

In order to do your best on a test, you need to be psyched up for it. Being psyched up helps you focus all your attention on studying for and taking a test. For most of us, neither activity is fun, but when we realize that tests are the way we are evaluated in school and that we have to pass them in order to succeed, then we can psych up and go!

How do professional athletes and actors and executives psych themselves up? Studies of highly successful people have shown that their ability to keep their ultimate goals in mind is the key to their success.

You too can psych yourself up for a test by visualizing your ultimate goal and thinking about how the test is connected to it. Here are some questions to help you make that connection. Try answering them when it is time to get ready for your next test.

1. What is my ultimate goal in life?

   _____

   _____

2. Why am I going to school?

   _____

   _____

3. What relationship does school have with my ultimate goal?

   _____

   _____

4. Is a good grade on this test important to my final grade in the class?

   _____

5. Is a good grade in this class important to my success in school?

   _____

6. Is a good grade in this class important to my getting a degree?

   _____

7. Is a good grade in this class necessary to my qualifying for the advanced program of my choice?

8. Is a good grade in this class important to further my professional or career interests?

_____

9. Will it be worthwhile to invest some time studying in order to get a good test grade?

_____

10. Do I believe that if I set my mind to something, I can do it?

_____

11. Do I have the ability to perform well on this test if I am prepared?

_____

Relaxing

Once you are psyched up, you are ready to organize a game plan and get to work. But you need to know how to keep yourself from getting too much on edge. You want to be psyched up to work, but you don't want to be so strung out that you get nothing accomplished. Remember, it is normal to feel anxious about tests, and anxiety can help you work harder and concentrate better—as long as you keep it under control. You are aiming for high productivity—*consistently* high. To do your best, you need to be highly motivated, but not panicked.

In this section of the chapter, you will discover that the best way to do this is to plan your schedule several days before a test so you will be able to get enough sleep, some physical exercise, and some quiet leisure time—and have enough time to study as well. Then you will learn some relaxation techniques and other ways to stay calm on the day of the test. Go over the material in this section now so that you are familiar with it. Prior to preparing for a test, you might want to review this material on relaxation if you feel you are getting too anxious.

Getting in Shape for a Test

Sleep is important. Staying up all night to study is usually not wise. It is more beneficial to get your normal eight (or six or ten) hours of sleep each night than to try to compensate for an all-nighter by sleeping late the next day. You need to be alert when you study for a test and alert when you take a test. Regular sleep habits increase your chance of a good night's rest, and getting up at about the same time every morning means that you won't have to rush to fit everything into the day's schedule.

It should be noted here, however, that staying up all night to complete an important paper is acceptable once in a while—if that's the only way to finish and if the all-nighter is not too close to test-preparation days. Staying up all night to finish a paper can be an efficient use of your time because you are accomplishing an academic goal. You will be judged on your performance, which in this case is the paper. For a test, however, your performance takes place in school at the time of the test, and you must be alert to do your best. It doesn't matter how alert you are after a term-paper all-nighter, as long as you don't miss important lecture notes or sleep through a test-preparation day. This book is not advocating staying up all night for every paper, but if, on occasion, the only way you can finish a paper and have prime hours available to study for a test, too, is to do an all-nighter, then that is the best use of your time.

In addition to regular sleep habits, taking occasional breaks from studying for quiet leisure activities and for physical exercise will also help you to stay alert. Physical activities such as running, tennis, or handball are good tension-breakers as long as they are part of your usual activities. If you do not normally participate in strenuous physical exercise, don't start when you are studying for a test. Instead, try a brisk walk or some moderate stretching to relieve tension.

Allow some quiet relaxation time as well in order to reduce fatigue and tension. Use mealtimes as breaks from the rigors of studying, and then spend a little more time in conversation, reading for pleasure, watching a movie or television show, or listening to music. Relaxing after a meal not only helps to reduce tension, but it also improves digestion, which contributes to better health. Moreover, you are not as alert right after a meal, so studying then is not as effective as half an hour or an hour later.

A study break—whether physical activity or quiet relaxation—should be a reward for hard work. Stop studying as soon as you feel you are becoming overly fatigued. This does not mean the moment you feel a little tired. Push yourself a little further by thinking of your reward—and stop for a break when you have pushed yourself to the limit of your concentration.

What kinds of relaxation breaks do you find most appealing? List some here and use them as rewards for hard studying.

_____

_____

_____

_____

_____

The activities you have just listed should be used for study breaks, not distraction. Anything that competes for your attention while you are preparing for a test should be avoided. Radios, stereos, television, the telephone, and other distractions should be reserved for relaxation breaks.

Staying Calm on Exam Day

Knowing that you are testwise—that you have followed your game plan to study for the test and that you know all the techniques for taking essay and objective tests—will make you feel more confident. But even testwise students can become overly nervous just before and during a test. If this happens to you, be sure you know some proven ways to offset nervousness before it gets too serious and you lose control.

Some students who frequently experience test panic are helped by relaxation training. Some school and college counselors have training materials, usually on tape, that teach relaxation techniques. (If your counselor does not have relaxation training materials, he or she can probably tell you where you can get them or can suggest some beneficial relaxation techniques.) The basic concept of all relaxation techniques is that if you can relax physically, it is not possible to be overly anxious mentally. The training materials teach you to relax whenever you wish, and with a bit of practice you can learn to relax while taking exams.

Relaxation Techniques

There are a great many relaxation techniques. Here are a few easy ones to begin with.

- Inhale deeply with your eyes closed, hold your breath, and then exhale slowly. Do this several times if you need to.
- Sit back in your chair and get as comfortable as possible. If your shoes feel uncomfortable, slip them off; no one will notice your feet under the desk or table. Try loosening your entire body. Close your eyes for a few moments; you should feel more calm and relaxed.
- Tighten all your muscles from head to toe, and hold them. Then let all your muscles loosen.
- Tighten your muscles and then systematically (toes to feet to ankles to calves to knees and so on) loosen each part of your body.

Practice these relaxation techniques before the test so you will be familiar with them at exam time. Then repeat these tension-breakers as often as necessary during the test.

In addition to these relaxation techniques, there are a number of other things you can do just before and during a test to keep anxiety at a minimum.

1. *Get a good night's sleep.* Even though cramming will be recommended later in the book as a test-preparation technique, it doesn't necessarily mean staying up all night before a test!

2. *Eat some breakfast or lunch before the test,* but avoid greasy foods and foods with high acidity. Having food in your stomach may help calm nervousness and give you energy. But don't overeat, because that could make you sluggish and sleepy.

3. *Allow yourself the necessary time to get to the place of the test.* If you are already nervous, rushing will only make you more so.

4. *Don't stand around and talk to others* just before going in to take the test. They may confuse you or make you nervous about your preparation. Instead, use those precious moments before the test to quietly review your condensed notes. (Techniques for condensing your notes will be explained in Chapter 3.)

5. Review Chapter 6 so you will *be ready when you enter the testing room* and will know just how to proceed.

6. *Don't panic if others are busily writing and you are not.* Your thinking and organizing may be more profitable than their writing. You will have your own strategies for taking the test.

7. *Don't be upset if other students finish their tests before you do.* Use as much time as you are allowed. Remember, you are prepared. Students who leave early may not be testwise and are not always the best-prepared students.

8. If you feel very tense during the test, *remind yourself that you are a player in this game.* Stress is part of it; you will hold up well under the stress. You will play the game and do it well; then you will be able to leave and give yourself a reward for a game well played.

Organizing Your Course Content

All of the information in this chapter about getting in the proper frame of mind for tests and all the information in the rest of the book about studying for and taking tests will be of little use without a thorough knowledge and understanding of the contents of the course that come from lecture notes and reading. So the rest of this chapter will be devoted to suggestions for making your course contents useful test-study resources.

Lecture Notes

When it comes time to study for a test, a thorough set of lecture notes will be essential. (Chapter 3 will provide techniques for using your notes to study for a test.) Your care in note-taking from the very first day of class is crucial for later test-taking preparation. Here are some tips to help you build an orderly and thorough set of notes.

1. *Go to all classes* and take notes on everything the instructor emphasizes. If possible, sit as close to the instructor as you can so you can hear and see everything.

2. *Be a good listener.* Be alert to what the instructor is saying as you are taking notes. You have to train yourself to concentrate on what is currently being said while recording ideas that have already been said.

3. *Keep notes for each course separate* from notes for the other courses. This is easier if you use a loose-leaf binder or file folder rather than a spiral-bound notebook. You want to be able to reorganize your note pages and add handouts later when you study for tests.

4. *Take notes on one side of the page only,* and record the name or number of the course and the date on each page.

5. *Use standard-size notebook paper.* Try to leave spaces between topics as they change. (You'll find an example of class notes in Chapter 3 on pages 47–49.)

6. *Make your notes complete and clear* enough so they will have meaning later. You should not write in full sentences; phrases are fine, but be sure that they make sense to you and that you have the whole idea.

7. *If you missed something important, stay after class* and ask the instructor about it so you can fill in the gap in your notes.

8. *Write legibly.*

9. *Develop abbreviations* of common words and recurring terms so you can save time while taking lecture notes.

10. *Use a symbol,* such as an asterisk (*), to mark the points the instructor emphasizes.

11. *Keep assignments or suggestions for readings separate from lecture notes* but close enough to indicate which lecture they were related to. One good place is at the end of your notes on each topic.

12. *If ideas or examples come to mind* as the instructor lectures, *jot them down*—but label them "me" or identify them in some other way so you won't get your thoughts mixed in with the instructor's words.

13. *Be alert for clues to test items.* Sometimes the instructor will say, "This is important," or "I might ask you this on a test," or "You will see this again." You might want to asterisk and underline these items in your notes.

14. *Always record your instructor's examples exactly as they are given.* They might turn up again in similar form on a test.

15. *Copy all charts, diagrams, and lists* exactly as your instructor puts them on the chalkboard.

16. *Stay to the end of the class and keep taking notes to the end.* Sometimes instructors run out of time and will crowd half the planned lecture into the last five minutes.

17. *Don't rely on a friend to take notes for you* unless you have to be absent. The notes may not be good, or even if they are, they may not

trigger the same information to you as they do to someone else. Therefore, they will not be as effective as notes you take for yourself.

18. *If you are absent, do copy someone's notes.* Try picking someone in class who takes good notes and knows what is going on. Read over the notes. If you do not understand something, ask the instructor first. If you can't ask the instructor, then ask the person who took the notes.

19. *At the end of the day, go over your notes from all of your classes.* Fill in the places that seem incomplete; in a week, your memory of the lecture won't be as clear. Wherever possible, it is an excellent idea to label your notes for each class by topics covered during the lecture.

20. If the instructor gives out any handouts with a lecture, *label the handouts with the course name or number and date.* Later, group those handouts with the appropriate lecture notes by punching holes in the handouts and putting them behind the notes in your binder or folder.

Textbooks and Outside Readings

If at all possible, keep up with your assigned textbook and outside readings. There may come a time, however, when too much work comes all at once. Don't panic; instead complete as many of the steps listed in the box "How to Read a Textbook Step-by-Step" as your time allows. That way, you'll have at least some degree of familiarity with the material.

✓To *quickly survey* your assigned textbook chapters or other readings and get an idea of the content, follow Steps 1 through 5. If you have time, *skim* the chapters to get a more detailed picture of their contents as directed in Step 6. Step 7 tells you how to *read* the assignment. Step 8 tells how to *take notes* on your reading for test preparation after you have read each chapter section. Steps 7 and 8 would have to be omitted if you have a whole textbook to read in only a few days. The chapter notes you collect in Step 8 can be valuable review material prior to chapter, unit, midterm, and final exams.

How to Read a Textbook Step-by-Step

Step 1: Pictures. Go through the entire chapter and look at all the pictures, tables, charts, diagrams, graphs, maps, and other illustrations. Read any written notations under or above the illustration for clarification and read all the information in tables, charts, and other illustrations containing statistical data.

Step 2: Introduction. Most well-written chapters have an introduction. This will usually be the first few paragraphs. Read the introductory paragraphs to each assigned chapter and try asking yourself the factual questions that a reporter asks—who? what? where? when?—and the inferential questions that a reporter asks—why? and how?

Step 3: Bold Print. Read all the bold print from the beginning to the end of the chapter or selection. Very often, the bold print serves as an outline of the chapter.

Step 4: Summary. Most well-written chapters have a summary or some type of wrap-up paragraphs. These will usually be at the very end of the chapter. Read the summary paragraphs.

Step 5: Questions. If there are questions or points for discussion in the chapter or at the end, read them over. These questions will often be clues about the most important information in the chapter.

Step 6: Skim. Starting at the beginning of the chapter, read the first and last sentence of each paragraph. The first sentence is usually a key one. The last sentence usually wraps up a thought and ties it in with the first sentence of the next paragraph. After reading the first sentence in a paragraph, skim through the following sentences until you come to the first word of the last sentence and then read that sentence.

Step 7: Read. Starting at the beginning of the chapter, read it all the way through. Whenever you come to the bold print, turn it into a question and read to answer that question.

Step 8: Note-taking. Fold a sheet of loose-leaf paper in half vertically. On the left half of the paper write the bold-faced headings from the chapter. On the right half write a few key words or phrases that will answer the questions you asked from the bold print in Step 7 as well as any words, phrases, or ideas that might be a test item.

Chapter Summary

It is normal to be nervous to a certain degree at test time. No matter how well prepared you are, you will still feel some tension. Don't be alarmed by it. Remember, even the professional actor, lawyer, football player, runner, and business executive feel tense before a big event. They let their tension work for them and help them sharpen their performance. You can do the same. If you prepared well for the test, which is your big event, you will do well because you are testwise.

You know how to psych yourself up because you can see the connection between your ultimate goal in life and the test. You know how to relax when you get too tense because you schedule your study time before a test to allow for leisure-time rewards and because you use relaxation techniques. And you know how to organize your course content by keeping thorough, systematic class notes and by reading your assignments for content step-by-step.

Chapter 2

Developing a Game Plan

Time management is a basic survival skill in school. Time management means that you decide which tasks are most and least important and then schedule your time accordingly. This planning provides structure to your studying, frees you from uncertainty and guilt, and saves time by helping you not waste time. Decisions about how much time to spend studying for a test and what is most important to study constitute your game plan—an essential part of being testwise.

This chapter is filled with forms to help you figure out your study schedule and to help you decide what is most important to study in a limited amount of time. While they may seem like extra work at first, after you've practiced using them in this chapter, you will find that they save you time and make your studying more efficient. (An extra copy of each of the forms is included in the Appendix at the back of the book.)

Master Test Schedule for the Term

The first step in preparing for a test is developing a schedule of all the test dates for all the classes you are taking this term—with a brief description of the content of each test (if you know). If an exam is an especially important one, like a midterm or a final, note that with the exam date and circle it on your schedule. It is a good idea to fill out the schedule in pencil, since instructors sometimes change dates, cancel tests, and schedule new ones. Sometimes they do not give their exam schedule for the entire term at the beginning of the course, so you need to keep your master test schedule handy in order to keep it up-to-date.

Horatio's

Master Test Schedule for Term

Test Dates & Content	English	Biology	Math	Psychology		
Course Names						
Week 1	9/26 Vocab.					
Week 2	10/3 Vocab.		10/1 Chs. 1-3			
Week 3	10/10 Vocab.			10/7 Unit 1		
Week 4	10/17 Vocab.		10/15 Chs. 4-6			
Week 5	10/24 Vocab.		(10/24) midterm: Chs. 1-6	10/21 Unit 2		
Week 6	(10/27) midterm: Vocab. + Lit. (Chs. 1-9)	(10/31) midterm: Chs. 1-8				
Week 7	11/7 Vocab.		11/5 Chs. 7-9			
Week 8	11/14 Vocab.			11/11 Unit 3		
Week 9	11/21 Vocab.		11/19 Chs. 10-12			
Week 10				11/25 Unit 4		
Week 11						
Week 12						
Week 13						
Week 14						
Week 15						
Week 16						
Finals Week	(12/10) Vocab. + Lit. Book (Chs. 1-18)	(12/5) Chs. 9-15	(12/8) Chs. 7-12	(12/11) Units 1-4		

Before you attempt to fill out your master test schedule for the term (page 21), look at the sample master test schedule for a student we will call Horatio (see page 18). He attends a school that uses the quarter system. Since there are only ten weeks in the term plus finals' week, Horatio has crossed out Weeks 11–16 on his master schedule.

Looking at Horatio's test schedule, see if you can answer the planning question in Exercise 2.1. (Answers can be found at the back of the book.)

Exercise 2.1

1. What is the date of Horatio's first test this term?

_____

2. Which class is it for?

_____

3. What is the content of that first test?

_____

4. Is it a major test?

_____

5. During Week 5, Horatio has three tests. For which classes?

_____

6. (a) His schedule indicates that two of the tests in Week 5 are on the same day. Which two?

_____

(b) Of the tests on the same day, which one should Horatio spend most of his time studying for and why?

_____

_____

7. List the order of the tests that Horatio should study for during Week 6 of the term.

_____

8. During Weeks 2, 3, 4, 7, 8, and 9, Horatio always has two minor tests scheduled. One of the tests is always in _____ . During any one of those weeks, does he have more than one test in one day?

_____

9. Which test do you consider more important during Week 2? _____

during Week 3? _____   during Week 4? _____

during Week 7? _____   during Week 8? _____

during Week 9? _____

Why are these the most important weekly tests?

_____

_____

10. (a) List in order the tests that Horatio should study for during finals week.

_____

(b) Which two finals will cover the most material?

_____

(c) Which finals will cover only material that came after the midterm test?

_____

After you have compared your answers to Exercise 2.1 with those in the back of the book, fill out your master test schedule for this term (page 21). (An extra form is provided in the Appendix for future use.) Remember to use pencil, to include specific dates and content, and to circle your midterms, finals, and any other major tests you may have.

Master Test Schedule for Term

Test Dates & Content	Course Names					
Week 1						
Week 2						
Week 3						
Week 4						
Week 5						
Week 6						
Week 7						
Week 8						
Week 9						
Week 10						
Week 11						
Week 12						
Week 13						
Week 14						
Week 15						
Week 16						
Finals Week						

Planning for Each Test

Now that you have an overview of your test schedule for the term, you can begin deciding how much and what to study for each test. Getting organized to study for a test is an essential part of being testwise. This is the time to anticipate what may possibly be on the test and to decide what you will have to study. The first step in getting organized is to answer the following questions.

1. What do I already know about the topics?
2. What don't I know about the topics?
3. What clarifications do I need from my instructor?
4. What materials do I need to assemble to study?
5. What outside research do I need to do?
6. What reading do I still need to do?
7. What information seems most important?
8. How much time should I allow to prepare adequately for each area?
9. How much time do I actually have?
10. What is my game plan?

In the remainder of this chapter, you will learn how to do a test analysis and use files of old tests in order to be able to answer questions 1–7; you will learn how to make a study schedule for a test in order to make the answer to question 9 come as close as possible to the answer to 8; and you will learn how to make a daily list of things to do to prepare for a test. Together, the study schedule, the test analysis, and the list of things to do make up your game plan—the answer to question 10.

Test Analysis

It is very important to know as much as possible about a test in order to plan your study schedule and preparation strategies. Use any opportunities your instructor gives to ask questions concerning a test. Sometimes instructors will even schedule special review sessions before a major test. Using a test analysis form (pages 28–29) during these sessions is another way to predict the content and format of a test.

Even without a review session, however, you can obtain most of the information to complete a test analysis form through your classes and your readings. You should fill out a test analysis form (photocopy the blank one in the Appendix or make your own) for each test you will take during the term. Even though the form may at first seem to be a lot of extra trouble, it will be worth it when you get ready to study.

Be sure to fill in all the information you can get about a test on the form. Some of the blanks can be filled in from your class notes and handouts. Often after taking the first test for a class, you will have more information about what to expect on the rest. For example, it is probable that the vocabulary tests that Horatio will take in English during Weeks 2–5 and Weeks 7–9 will be a lot like the vocabulary test he took in Week 1. And the format for his psychology unit tests in Weeks 5, 8, and 10 is likely to resemble that of the Unit 1 test given in the third week of the term. It is best not to assume they will all be exactly the same, however; you should ask your instructor.

Knowing the format of the test is highly valuable. Objective tests mean that you will have to be able to recognize answers, and many of them will be specific facts. Subjective, or essay, tests mean that you will have to have an overall understanding of the content and be able to cite some specifics; you will have to generate the answers yourself rather than just recognize them. Knowing the total number of items on the test, the material to be covered, and the number of questions on each area of content will help you decide how to focus your studying and how to budget your study time. Comparing the number of questions to the time allowed will let you know whether you will have to have quick recall or can take time to think. If you know who is writing and grading the test, you can anticipate particular biases—such as requiring correct spelling or preferring brief answers—and study accordingly.

What to Ask Your Instructor.   Ask questions only about things that you really need to know and that have not already been answered in class. Very often, if you listen attentively, instructors will intentionally or inadvertently tell you a lot about an upcoming test as they lecture. You cannot expect them to give you the exact test questions, but often they will mention topics or chapters to study, specific areas of importance, or kinds of test questions to expect. A week or two before the test, they might also be willing to answer specific questions from your test analysis form; however, the test might not be written that far in advance.

When you ask your instructor about tests, be tactful. Keep in mind that some questions on the form should not be asked of the instructor. For example, the question on biases is one for you to answer based on what you have observed in class or what students who have already taken the course have told you; it is not a question you would ask the instructor.

Use Old-Test Files.   In addition to what you learn in class about an upcoming test, tests from previous terms can also help you anticipate the content and format of your test. Sometimes, schools and colleges have a file of old tests that are available for student review. They can usually be found in the library, the counselors' offices, or in a reading and study skills center, if your school has one. Ask your instructor and your counselor if there are files of old tests and where they can be found. Your instructor may even have copies of past exams for students to review.

If you do find some old exams, use them to identify your general strengths and weaknesses. Copying and memorizing the questions on old exams will not help much. Instead use them as guides to the type of test that may be given and the content that is likely to be emphasized.

In summary, use information from your class and from past exams to fill in the test analysis form. You may not be able to fill in every blank, but the more information you have, the better you will be able to anticipate the test and the better you will be able to study for it.

For an example of how a test analysis form can be filled out, take a look at the sample form for one of Horatio's tests (pages 25–26). Then answer the questions in Exercise 2.2 (compare your answers to those at the back of the book). After you have studied this sample form, you will be ready to fill out your own test analysis form for an upcoming test (pages 28–29). (Another blank form is included in the Appendix for your future use.)

Test Analysis for Individual Tests

Class _Psychology_   Instructor _Parker_

Date of Test _10/7_   Time of Day _1:15_

% of Grade _12½ %_   Major or Minor Test _Minor_

What is the *format* of the test?

Essay: ___✓___ Long-Answer (discuss, trace, compare and contrast)

     ___✓___ Short-Answer (list, name, define, identify)

Objective: _____ True-False

     _____ Multiple-Choice

     _____ Matching

     _____ Completion (fill-in-the-blank)

How many questions will be on the test? ___4___

How many of each kind of question will be on it?

___2___ Long-Answer Essay   _____ True-False

___2___ Short-Answer Essay   _____ Multiple-Choice

     _____ Matching

     _____ Completion

How much time will I have for the test? ___1 hour___

What is the *content* of the test? ___Unit 1___

Topics or Kinds of Problems	Sources of Content (notes, readings, labs)	% of Score and # of Questions	Format of Questions*
what is psychology and how is it diff. from psychiatry	Text: chap. 1 plus class notes	30%/1	Long-Answer Essay: discuss and contrast
history of psych. and four schools of psych.	Text: chap. 2 plus class notes	30%/1	Long-Answer Essay: trace and discuss
Major fields of psych.	Text: chap. 3 plus class notes	20%/1	Short-Answer Essay: identify and define
Methods of psych.	Text: chap. 4 plus class notes	20%/1	Short-Answer Essay: list and define

Are details or general concepts important? *both*

Do I have to know formulas or theorems? *No* If so, which ones?*

Do I have to know definitions? *Yes* If so, which ones?* *the major fields of psychology; the methods of psychology*

Do I have to know important names and dates? *Yes* If so, which ones? *for history of psych (time periods but not specific dates): Plato, Aristotle (early days), Hobbes, Locke (1600s); Wilhelm Wundt (1879)—structuralism; Watson, Pavlov (1913)—behaviorism; Wertheimer, Kohler, Koffka, Lewin (early 1900s)—Gestalt; Freud (early 1900s)—psychoanalysis*

Will points be taken off for spelling errors? *No, as long as word can be recognized*

Can I bring a dictionary to use during the test? *No*

Can I bring a calculator to use during the test? *Not Applicable*

If problems have to be worked out, how much credit is given for accuracy? *N.A.* and how much for method? *N.A.*

Will this be an open-book test? *No*

Are copies of previous exams available for inspection? *No*

Is this a departmental test or one made up by the instructor? *Instructor*

Who will grade this test?** *Instructor*

Do the writer and grader of this test have any special biases?**

Additional Clues or Notes:**

Be sure to emphasize everything we emphasized in class lectures when I answer questions.

Notes: * You may not be able to find this out before the test.
** You shouldn't ask this question of the instructor.

Exercise 2.2

1. The material that Horatio will have to study comes from two sources. What are they?

   _____

2. To prepare for this test, should Horatio refer to the sections in this book on objective tests?

   _____

3. (a) Which are the two most important areas of content for this test?

   _____

   _____

   (b) Why?

   _____

   _____

   (c) Which kinds of questions will be asked on these two most important areas?

   _____

   (d) Should Horatio spend more time studying these two areas than the others? Why?

   _____

   _____

   _____

4. Will Horatio have to do much memorizing for this test?

   _____

   What are some of the things he will have to memorize?

   _____

   _____

   _____

5. When studying for the test, should Horatio concentrate on his class notes?

   _____

Test Analysis for Individual Tests

Class _____   Instructor _____

Date of Test _____   Time of Day _____

% of Grade _____   Major or Minor Test _____

What is the *format* of the test?

    Essay: _____ Long-Answer (discuss, trace, compare and contrast)

                  _____ Short-Answer (list, name, define, identify)

    Objective: _____ True-False

                  _____ Multiple-Choice

                  _____ Matching

                  _____ Completion (fill-in-the-blank)

How many questions will be on the test? _____

How many of each kind of question will be on it?

_____ Long-Answer Essay   _____ True-False

_____ Short-Answer Essay   _____ Multiple-Choice

                                    _____ Matching

                                    _____ Completion

How much time will I have for the test? _____

What is the *content* of the test? _____

Topics or Kinds of Problems	Sources of Content (notes, readings, labs)	% of Score and # of Questions	Format of Questions*
_____	_____	_____	_____
_____	_____	_____	_____
_____	_____	_____	_____
_____	_____	_____	_____
_____	_____	_____	_____
_____	_____	_____	_____

Are details or general concepts important? _____

Do I have to know formulas or theorems? _____ If so, which ones?* _____

_____

Do I have to know definitions? _____ If so, which ones?* _____

_____

Do I have to know important names and dates? _____ If so, which ones? _____

_____

_____

_____

Will points be taken off for spelling errors? _____

Can I bring a dictionary to use during the test? _____

Can I bring a calculator to use during the test? _____

If problems have to be worked out, how much credit is given for accuracy? _____ and how

much for method? _____

Will this be an open-book test? _____

Are copies of previous exams available for inspection? _____

Is this a departmental test or one made up by the instructor? _____

Who will grade this test?** _____

Do the writer and grader of this test have any special biases?** _____

_____

Additional Clues or Notes:**

_____

_____

_____

Notes: * You may not be able to find this out before the test.
       ** You shouldn't ask this question of the instructor.

Study Schedules for Each Test

A study schedule will ensure that you will have time to prepare yourself thoroughly and efficiently for a test. The schedule will help you decide priorities for study and make commitments to yourself. When planning your schedule for test preparation, you will need to decide when to start studying and how much to study. To make these decisions, answer the following questions:

1. How much time is available to study for this test?
2. Where do I stand now in the class and how important is the test? How good a grade do I need on this test?
3. How much time does the test analysis form indicate that I will need in order to study adequately for the test?

How Much Time Is Available?   In order to develop a study schedule for a test, you first need to see how much time is not already committed in the two weeks before the test. After you have crossed out the hours when you will be going to class, working, doing out-of-class assignments and papers, and sleeping, the hours left are those available for studying for a test.

To see what a study schedule looks like, turn to pages 31 and 32 for Horatio's study schedule the week before and the week of his psychology exam. Note that the only activities with a label are his tests; for all other activities, the hours have simply been crossed out. The blank hours are those available for studying for the test.

Looking at Horatio's schedules, we can see that during the week of his psychology test he also has a test in English, but it is three days after his psychology test. Since the vocabulary test is a minor one and he has study time available for it, he doesn't need to worry about studying for it until after his psychology test. The week before the psychology exam, Horatio has a math test on Wednesday and a vocabulary test on Friday. It looks like he will need to use his test study time that week (through Friday) getting ready for those two tests. Thus, the time that Horatio has available to study for the psychology exam is the hours on Saturday, Sunday, Monday afternoon and evening, and Tuesday morning.

On pages 33 and 34 there are blank schedules for the week before and the week of the exam. Cross out the hours for your fixed activities—including paper writing and sleeping—so you can see how much total time you have to study for your next major exam. Be sure to write in all the other tests that you will have to take during those two weeks, too. (Another pair of schedules is included in the Appendix for your future use.)

Schedule: Week Before _Psychology_ Test

Hour	Mon.	Tues.	Wed.	Thurs.	Fri.	Sat.	Sun.
A.M.							
12–1							
1–2							
2–3							
3–4							
4–5							
5–6							
6–7							
7–8							
8–9							
9–10					Vocab. Test		
10–11							
11–12			Math Test				
P.M.							
12–1							
1–2							
2–3							
3–4							
4–5							
5–6							
6–7							
7–8							
8–9							
9–10							
10–11							
11–12							

Schedule: Week of _____*Psychology*_____ Test

Hour	Mon.	Tues.	Wed.	Thurs.	Fri.	Sat.	Sun.
A.M.							
12–1							
1–2							
2–3							
3–4							
4–5							
5–6							
6–7							
7–8							
8–9							
9–10					*Vocab. Test*		
10–11							
11–12							
P.M.							
12–1							
1–2		*Psych Test*					
2–3							
3–4							
4–5							
5–6							
6–7							
7–8							
8–9							
9–10							
10–11							
11–12							

Schedule: Week Before _____ Test

Hour	Mon.	Tues.	Wed.	Thurs.	Fri.	Sat.	Sun.
A.M.							
12–1							
1–2							
2–3							
3–4							
4–5							
5–6							
6–7							
7–8							
8–9							
9–10							
10–11							
11–12							
P.M.							
12–1							
1–2							
2–3							
3–4							
4–5							
5–6							
6–7							
7–8							
8–9							
9–10							
10–11							
11–12							

Schedule: Week of _____ Test

Hour	Mon.	Tues.	Wed.	Thurs.	Fri.	Sat.	Sun.
A.M.							
12–1							
1–2							
2–3							
3–4							
4–5							
5–6							
6–7							
7–8							
8–9							
9–10							
10–11							
11–12							
P.M.							
12–1							
1–2							
2–3							
3–4							
4–5							
5–6							
6–7							
7–8							
8–9							
9–10							
10–11							
11–12							

How Good a Grade Do I Need on This Test?   Now that you have counted the hours you have available to study for your next major test, you need to consider where you stand in that class, how much the test counts, and how important a good grade on the test will be. Figure out your course average before the test, and then refer to your test analysis form to see how much the test counts toward your final grade in the course. Generally, the lower your course average and the more important the test, the more important it is to try for a high grade and to spend more hours studying. Conversely, the higher your course average and the less important the test, the less important it is to use all available hours to study for it.

How Much Time Do I Need to Study Adequately?   Look at your test analysis form to see what will be covered on the test. Next, assess where you are right now in terms of readings, other assignments, labs, and problems that must be completed for that test. Here are seven steps to follow to make that assessment.

1. *List the required readings* that will be covered by the test.
2. *Check off* those that you have done.
3. *List any other required assignments, labs, or problems* on which the test may be based.
4. *Check off* those that you have done.
5. *Look at what still needs to be done* before you can begin to study.
6. *Try to determine how much of the test will come from the work you still need to do.*
7. *Figure out how much time it will take* you to do that work.

If you have a lot of work still to complete but not enough available study hours to do it as well as to study for the test properly, you will need to find some ways to cut corners to complete the readings and other assignments. For example, you can use Steps 1–5 from Chapter 1 (page 15) to quickly survey the readings and get an overall idea of their content. Or you can skim the problems left to do, and, if there is more than one using a particular concept or theorem, work only one. Based on how much of the test will come from these incomplete assignments, decide how much time you will spend on them.

Through this decision-making process, you will be setting priorities; some parts of the content need more time than others. You will need some flexibility in your study schedule, too, in case a particular reading assignment or problem turns out to be more difficult than you had at first assumed. Don't forget to allow some time, too, for social activities and study breaks. In short, be reasonable in planning your study schedule; a study plan that demands every minute of every available hour will be impossible to live up to. Being a testwise student is not easy; it involves not only commitment and persistence but also good judgment—that is, knowing which material to focus on and which to review lightly or to even ignore.

Planning Test-Study Time

When Horatio looks at the test analysis form for his psychology test (pages 25–26), he sees that he has done only half the required reading for the test and still has to read Chapters 3 and 4 in his textbook. Each chapter and his class notes on them will constitute 20 percent of the test, so they are important. Although this is not a major test and accounts for only 12½ percent of his final grade in the course, Horatio decides it will be important to try to do well because it is the first test in the class. He knows that first impressions count and wants the instructor to consider him a good student.

Looking at his schedules for the week before and the week of the test (pages 31–32), he notes that the open times on Saturday, Sunday, Monday, and Tuesday before the test are the only hours he has to prepare for the test. Horatio decides to use the study time available on Saturday to read Chapters 3 and 4 and take notes to answer test questions from those chapters. He will also go through his class notes on those chapters so he can fill in gaps with text notes. He plans to use the available time on Sunday to go back to Chapters 1 and 2 and take notes to help answer the test questions on those chapters. He will also look over the class notes he has on those chapters. (In Chapters 3–5, you will learn more about the techniques for studying readings and class notes that Horatio is planning to use.)

Studies of students preparing for tests have shown that the most important study time is the day and night before the test. Although long-range preparation and keeping up with class work is important, the material reviewed and recited the day and night before an exam will be remembered better than material reviewed earlier. Horatio is saving this most important time for reviewing and reciting. On Monday, he will study for the test by going back over all his notes and then writing answers to the questions he anticipates will be on the test. On Tuesday morning he will review again so that all the information will be fresh in his mind when he walks in to take the test at 1:15 P.M. that day.

On page 37, you will find the list Horatio has made of the things he needs to do to study for his psychology test, which includes the times when he plans to do them. Read over Horatio's list and then make one for your study time for your next test, using the test analysis form you filled out on pages 28–29 and the schedules on pages 33–34. (You will find another things-to-do form in the Appendix for your future use.)

Horatio's Things-to-Do-List

Things to Do to

Study for _Psychology_ Test

	Day or Date	Time
Read Ch. 3 in text	Sat.	9:00 – 10:30 A.M.
Read ch. 4 in text	Sat.	2:00 – 3:30 P.M.
Take notes on chs. 1-4 to		
answer test questions:		
Ch. 1	Sun.	9:00 – 10:00 A.M.
Ch. 2	Sun.	Noon – 1:00 P.M.
Ch. 3	Sat.	11:00 A.M. – Noon
Ch. 4	Sat.	4:00 – 5:00 P.M.
Go back over notes on all		
chapters (class & text)		
to answer test questions:		
Ch. 1	Sun.	10:30 – 11:30 A.M.
Ch. 2	Sun.	1:30 – 2:30 P.M.
Ch. 3	Sat.	12:30 – 1:30 P.M.
Ch. 4	Sat.	5:30 – 7:00 P.M.
Write an answer to each		
test question for:		
Ch. 1	Mon.	1:00 – 2:00 P.M.
Ch. 2	Mon.	2:15 – 3:15 P.M.
Ch. 3	Mon.	3:30 – 4:30 P.M.
Ch. 4	Mon.	4:45 – 5:45 P.M.
Take notes on each of		
the answers	Mon.	7:00 – 9:00 P.M.
Memorize notes on each		
of the answers	Tues.	8:00 – 10:00 A.M.
Read over answers one		
more time	Tues.	10:00 – 11:00 A.M.
Recite and cram from notes	Tues.	11:00 A.M. – Noon
Leave for school	Tues.	Noon
Arrive at school	Tues.	12:45 P.M.
Recite and cram from notes	Tues.	12:45 – 1:15 P.M.

Things-to-Do-List

Things to Do to

Study for _____ Test   Day or Date   Time

To make sure that he will complete each day's allotment of things to do, Horatio breaks down his game plan for test study into daily lists of things to do and writes each day's list on an index card to carry with him wherever he goes during the day. Before going to bed the night before a day of test preparation, Horatio will make a list of the things that have to be accomplished the next day and number them in the order they need to be done. The next day he will cross off each item after he completes it. If he does not finish everything on the card, he can put the tasks left to do at the top of the next day's card. Writing each day's tasks on a card is a motivational device because it not only forces Horatio to specify study time but also causes him to make a commitment to himself to complete each study task. If he does not finish everything on the list, he is likely to feel guilty.

Look at Horatio's daily list for Saturday, his first day of test preparation (page 40), and then make your own daily lists on index cards based on your things-to-do list (page 38). Use the box on page 40 for your first card.

Planning for Midterms and Finals

To prepare for these major tests, you should generally follow the planning and scheduling procedures already described in this chapter. There are a couple of differences, however. Because there are so many major tests within days of each other, you should allow two to three, rather than one to two, weeks to study. And you will have to establish more-detailed priorities for what you need to accomplish. (Note: A two-weeks-before-test schedule-planning form is included in the Appendix.)

Since you are under pressure to work especially hard for midterms and finals, you will need to use special decision-making strategies to get through them with the best grades possible. Here are some tips to use during the two to three weeks before midterms and finals.

1. *Follow all the organizing, evaluation, and planning strategies* described in this book.
2. *Figure out what your present grade is* in each class.
3. Look at your test analysis forms and all available past exams for each major test and *estimate how much time will be needed to prepare* for each of them. Which tests will require more effort and which ones less?
4. *Figure out how much catch-up work needs to be done* for each class. Plan to do catch-up work only on content you think will be on the exams.
5. *Rank these big tests* in order of importance.
6. Use that ranking to *set priorities for catching-up and studying for your exams.*
7. Starting two to three weeks before the tests, *catch up with the readings and other course work* according to your priorities.

8. Two weeks before the tests, *begin studying your class notes, readings, and other assignments.*

9. *Follow the procedures for studying* for the specific kinds of exams described in Chapters 3–5.

10. *Follow the procedures for taking* the specific kinds of exams described in Chapters 6–8.

Horatio's Daily List

Saturday
1. Look at test question for Ch. 3.
2. Read Ch. 3 to answer question.
   Take notes to answer question.
3. Go back over class notes to answer Ch. 3 question.
4. Group ch. notes and class notes on Ch. 3.
5. Look at test question for Ch. 4.
6. Read Ch. 4 and take notes to answer question.
7. Go back over class notes to answer Ch. 4 question.
8. Group ch. notes and class notes on Ch. 4.

Your First Daily List

Chapter Summary

Testwise students know the importance of getting organized to take a test. They don't just plunge in haphazardly and hope for the best. They have a game plan for their study, which means that they

- meticulously think things through and organize for the test;
- break tasks down into smaller ones;
- decide the order in which the tasks will be done;
- set time limits for the completion of each task;
- attend to one thing at a time;
- build in relaxation rewards along the way; and
- learn relaxation-training techniques in preparation for exam time.

Game Plan Checklist

To make sure that your game plan for studying for each test is complete, check off the items in this list as you get them done. (Another game plan checklist is included in the Appendix.)

_____ 1. Did I prepare a *master test schedule* for the term, putting in all my test dates?

_____ 2. Did I cross out all my fixed commitments on the *schedules for one week before the test and the week of the test* (two weeks before midterm and final tests) and note when I have other tests during those weeks?

_____ 3. Did I figure out when I have *study time available* on these schedules for each test?

_____ 4. Did I prepare a *test analysis form* using information from class, from the instructor, and from other sources?

_____ 5. Have I checked to see if there are *past exams* available for review?

_____ 6. Using my test analysis form and past exams (if they were available), did I determine *the format of the test* so I know whether to prepare for objective or essay questions?

_____ 7. Using my test analysis form, did I assess *where I am right now in terms of readings* and other assignments related to the test?

_____ 8. Did I make a complete *list of things to do* to prepare for the test, putting the most important items first and planning when to do them according to the time available on my study schedule?

_____ 9. Am I going to break down the things-to-do list into *daily lists* on cards?

Once you have checked off all the items on the list, you are ready for the next step: preparing and studying for your test!

Part Two

Preparing for Tests

Chapter 3

Test-Study Techniques

For most of the tests you take, you are not allowed to refer to your notes or your textbook. So, to do well, you must have the important information in your memory. In this chapter you will learn how to organize your resources (class notes, readings, and other assignments) so you can make study notes to use for memorizing key facts and concepts. You'll also learn a number of ways to memorize as well as the importance of cramming (which is really last-minute memorizing and reviewing) just before a test. All these are techniques the testwise student uses to study for every kind of objective and essay test.

Memorizing

Your memory is like a computer. It stores information for later retrieval. Good memory is developed; it doesn't just happen. Material has to be read and reviewed, classified and organized, reviewed and condensed, and reviewed some more.

There are three faculties to the memory process: retention, recognition, and recall. *Retention* is the capacity for remembering. *Recall* means retrieving stored information from your memory bank. To recall information, you must depend on your memory alone, while to recognize information, you are given an aid, or a cue. Thus, *recognition* is easier than recall. A multiple-choice test uses recognition memory; you recognize the right answers because you have seen them before. An essay test requires recall memory. Not surprisingly, research indicates that students who prepare for essay exams do better than those who prepare for objective exams, even if the exam is an objective one. This difference might be caused by the need to recall, rather than to just recognize information, for essay exams. So the testwise student will study thoroughly—to really *know* the material—even for an objective test.

Thoroughly knowing the material means committing it to long-term rather than short-term memory. *Short-term memory* is fleeting and limited. An example of short-term memory is when you dial information to get a telephone number, mentally or verbally repeat the number, dial the number, and then forget it. The number was never internalized and stored. When new information is added to short-term memory, old information is pushed out.

Long-term memory internalizes and stores information within the mind for later use. Information that is particularly appealing and important goes into long-term memory. That information is often used and repeated and becomes part of the memory bank.

Most of the material that students have to learn for tests is not appealing nor important enough to easily become part of long-term memory. Instead, it usually falls into the same category as the phone number that was needed only once. Without repetition or concentrated reviewing and reciting, most material studied for a test will be pushed out of our memories rapidly. Consequently, repetition and reciting must be a part of our exam study procedure. You cannot store all of the material in your long-term memory, but through increased familiarity you will be able to retain most of it and to recall it during the exam.

Research indicates that overlearning and thoroughly mastering material improves recall of it. This means that you should go through the rigors of analyzing, categorizing, note-taking, predicting, practicing, and condensing all the material to be learned. Because research also shows that new learning often displaces what was previously studied, you will need to review and recite just before the exam. This prevents the material from being displaced before you need to use it.

Organizing Your Resources

The first step in memorizing the necessary information for your test is to collect all the textbooks, notes, library materials, and other resources you think might contain exam material. Carefully go through the information on your test analysis form and be sure you have all the resources together in the location where you will study. You need a quiet and private spot where you can spread your materials out and know they will be left undisturbed.

Once your materials are all together, you should begin to organize them. Mark pertinent pages in your text and other books with paper-clipped notes indicating the topics. Then go back and make a list of the pages you need to study the topic. Next, pull out all the pertinent class notes and try to organize them into groups for each of the exam topics you anticipate or into groups by topics covered in the class notes.

Exercise 3.1

On pages 47–49 you will find Horatio's notes from his psychology class. Organize them according to the following topics, which are based on his test analysis form.
1. What is psychology and how is it different from psychiatry?
2. History of psychology and four schools of psychology
3. Major fields of psychology
4. Methods of psychology

If you think that certain notes should be categorized under the topic "What is psychology and how is it different from psychiatry?" then write a 1 next to the notes. If you think that certain notes should be categorized under the topic "History of psychology and four schools of psychology," then write a 2 next to those notes, and so on. If you think that certain notes do not fit any of the categories that Horatio expects to be on his test, write N/A (not applicable) next to those notes; they need not be included with the notes to review and study. (Check your organization of these notes with the answers for Exercise 3.1 in the back of the book.)

Horatio's Psychology Class Notes

Abnormal Psych. — studies all forms of abnormal human behavior.

Clinical Psych. — deals with normal and abnormal behavior, and with indiv. psychol. adjustment to oneself and one's environment.

Comparative Psych. — studies behavior and abilities of different animal species.

Developmental Psych. — studies changes in human behavior from birth to old age.

Educational Psych. — applies the principles of psych. to the ed. process.

Psychology is the science that studies why human beings and animals behave as they do. The psychologist is interested in understanding the whole range of human experience.

Psychology is one of the behavioral sciences, like biology, sociology, and anthropology.

Psychiatry is a medical science dealing mostly with mental illness. Psychology studies all kinds of behavior, normal as well as abnormal. Psychiatrists are physicians with M.D. degrees and special training in the field of mental illness. Most psychologists have a Ph.D. or M.A. degree instead of medical school training.

1. Experiments — the experimental method enables a psychologist to control the conditions that determine the aspect of behavior being studied.
2. Natural Observation — the direct observation of human behavior in its natural environment.
3. Case Histories — collection of info. about an individual's past and present life.
4. Surveys — the psychol. interviews members of a group by written questionnaires or orally. The psychol. can pull the info. together and draw conclusions about average attitudes or behavior.

Psychological problems are often categorized by the terms: 1. neurosis, 2. psychosis, 3. paranoia, 4. schizophrenia, and 5. depression.

Behaviorism — Watson — 1913 — reaction against structuralism. Watson called for the study of the observable behavior of humans and animals — not of their experiences.
Gestalt Psychology — concerned with the organization of mental processes — we perceive organized patterns and the whole — Wertheimer, Kohler, Koffka, Lewin.
Psychoanalysis — Freud — early 1900s — developed a theory to explain why people become emotionally disturbed — people repress the needs and desires that are unacceptable to themselves or society.

Careers in Psychology — for info. write Amer. Psych. Assoc., 1200 17th St., N.W., Washington, D.C. 20036.

Industrial Psych. — applies psych. principles and techniques to the needs and problems of industry.

Physiological Psych. — concerned with relationships between behavior and the function of the nervous system.

Social Psych. — studies relationships among people in groups and the formation of public opinion.

Personality studies — studies the diff. characteristics of people and how these characteristics develop and can be measured.

Perception studies — studies the process by which patterns of environmental energies become known as objects, events, people, and other aspects of the world.

Structuralism — Wundt — thought main purpose of psych. was to describe and analyze conscious experience, including sensations, images, and feelings of which only the person himself is aware.

Making Study Notes

Once you have organized all your material by exam topic, you should read it through and take notes. As you take these notes, you will be reviewing and learning the material. Then you can use the notes to memorize the material. To facilitate memorization, cluster the facts and ideas into meaningful categories. There are several ways to do this, depending on which is most appropriate for the material you need to memorize: by topic on index cards, in lists in a steno pad, or in outlines or diagrams on notebook paper.

Topic Cards.   This method works especially well for foreign language and other vocabulary study. It is also excellent for natural and biological science material, where there are classification systems to learn. Each card should be labeled by exam topic. In this way you will be able to add or delete cards as needed; as you learn the material on a card, you can set it aside. You will also be able to rearrange the cards as needed while studying.

Lists.   Another good method of making study notes, especially when reviewing factual material, is lists. In a stenographer's notebook, write the general topic and subtopic in the left-hand column, and in the right-hand column make a list of all relevant concepts and facts you come across as you view your readings and lecture notes.

The following example uses Horatio's psychology notes on psychoanalysis to show how to make notes in a list on steno-pad paper.

Notes in a List

Schools of psychology: psychoanalysis	early 1900s Freud developed theory to explain why people become emotionally disturbed people repress needs/desires that are unacceptable to themselves or society

Outlines.   This method of making notes works best when relationships among sets of information are important. It can also help you gain a perspective of the relation of the whole to its components. When using an outline, list your topic as the major heading. Next divide your topic into its major subtopics. Each major subtopic will be a separate heading. For each separate heading further divide your subtopic into its parts. Under each of those parts list the pertinent details and supportive information. It doesn't matter what combination of Roman numerals, Arabic numerals, and letters you use, as long as the outline makes sense to you.

The following example uses Horatio's psychology notes on the difference between psychology and psychiatry to illustrate outlining.

Notes in an Outline

Difference Between Psychology and Psychiatry

I. Psychology
   A. Behavioral Science
      1. Studies why human beings and animals behave as they do
      2. Studies the whole range of human experience
         (a) Normal
         (b) Abnormal
   B. Psychologists usually have a Ph.D. or M.A. degree

II. Psychiatry
   A. Medical Science
      1. Deals with abnormal behavior of human beings
      2. Deals mostly with mental illness
   B. Psychiatrists are physicians with M.D.'s and special training in mental illness

Diagrams. When using the family tree, or diagram, method of taking notes, you are laying out the material in diagrammatic form. Put the topic or central idea in a box at the top of the page, and then link subtopics or subsections of associated information in boxes joined by straight lines. The location of these boxes and the lines connecting them will be determined by the relationships among the various components of information being noted.

The following example uses Horatio's psychology notes on Gestalt psychology to illustrate the diagram technique.

Notes in a Diagram

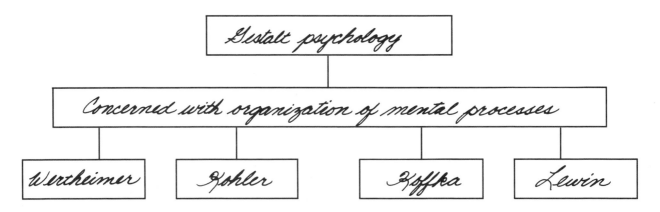

Condensing Study Notes

To memorize your study notes, it is helpful to condense them. The thinking and writing that you do to condense your already categorized notes is, in fact, part of the memorization process. Your primary objective, however, is to reduce your whole stack of notes for each topic into a smaller group covering the important specifics of each topic. After you've reduced your notes once, attempt to condense them even further. In effect, you are condensing your condensed notes. With each reduction you are absorbing more into your memory as well as getting a more workable set of notes for later review.

When condensing your study notes, you can use whatever system seems to work best for you: topic cards, lists, outlines, or diagrams. It is best to write your condensed notes on index cards because they are durable and easy to handle when memorizing and reciting. You can carry them with you to study during idle moments. This is an important convenience. Index cards can also be sorted easily and can be set aside when you are finished with any part of them.

Write your condensed notes on only one side of each card, and remember to keep the notes categorized all through the condensing process. How do you know when to stop condensing your notes? A good rule of thumb is to condense until they just about stop making sense.

Once your notes are condensed to their limit, you are ready to formally begin memorizing. Here are some ways to memorize the information in your condensed notes.

1. *Memorize and recite small groups of material.* Memorize your categorized cards one small group at a time. Recite what you've memorized, and set the cards aside. Go on to another small group of cards. Later, come back to the first group of memorized cards and review and recite again.

2. *Memorize what you don't know, but keep reviewing what you do know.* Spend most of the time studying the cards you aren't sure of. But periodically review and recite learned cards.

3. *Change the order of topics learned.* After you have been through all the topics at least once, shuffle the cards and study them again. If you are relying on the order of the topics as a memory cue, you may have trouble on the test, which will probably not use the same order.

Memorization Techniques

To memorize the information on your condensed study notes, there are a variety of techniques. Experiment with them, and use the ones that are most appropriate to the kind of information you are trying to memorize.

Memory Search and Association.   To memorize a specific piece of information, search your memory for anything in your past experience or knowledge that relates to it. If you can recall any related information, you probably can remember the new information by connecting it to what you already know.

For example, to remember the difference between the terms *inflation* and *depression* for an economics test, you might remember that inflating a tire makes it get bigger (with inflation, prices get bigger, or higher), while depression means feeling down (with depression, all economic activity slows down).

Mnemonic Connection.   Aid your memory by some artificial device or connection. Does a term sound or look like any word you already know? If so, make up an imaginary connection between the two. Or does the first syllable of the new term match the first syllable of any words you know that could be used as a connection? Or does the first letter of each word in a list or a group of words form an acronym, or a group of letters that you'll remember, to trigger your recall of the list? For example, to remember the title American Federation of Labor and Congress of Industrial Organizations, we use the acronym AFL-CIO. If you needed to remember the names of the Big Four allied countries during World War II, you could use the acronym GRUC (Great Britain, Russia, the United States, and China).

Often you can use a catchy phrase to help remember the order of something difficult to memorize. For example, for a music test, to recall the names and order of the notes on the lines of the treble clef staff, you could remember the phrase Every Good Boy Does Fine (E, G, B, D, F). For a physics exam, to recall the color code that signifies that value of electrical resistors, remember the phrase Big Bad Roy Goes Back Victorious Guzzling Wine (Black = 0; Brown = 1; Red = 2; Orange = 3; Yellow = 4; Green = 5; Blue = 6; Violet = 7; Gray = 8; White = 9).

Whole Learning. When there is a large, integrated body of facts and concepts, look over the material from beginning to end to see how it is related. Let your headings form the core of your study. Think how the material is interrelated. Look for principles, ideas, and concepts running through the material.

If you are memorizing a short poem, a piece of prose, a speech, a theorem, or a formula, repeat the whole thing over and over until memorized. If you are memorizing a long selection, divide it into two or three logical units. When they are learned, put them together and practice reciting the whole selection.

Recite and Write.   To promote recall, it is important to use some physical activity. Say aloud or write in your own words the ideas and facts you want to remember. Writing or reciting helps you transfer what might have been a fleeting piece of information into your memory bank. The amount of reciting or writing depends on the material. If lists of names, dates, or formulas are to be memorized, reciting or writing can take a considerable amount of time. If ideas, theories, or comparisons are to be memorized, reciting or writing will not be as time-consuming.

Cramming

The term *cramming* has a bad connotation because it is often used to refer to students who didn't take time to prepare for an exam earlier, and so must stay up most of the night before trying to do all the necessary studying. But the term can also refer to students who have been studying for an exam for several days and review, recite, and memorize their condensed notes just before going to bed—for a good night's sleep—before the exam.

Cramming can be an essential and desirable aspect of exam preparation. As already stressed, repetition, reviewing, and reciting are essential for memorization. Forgetting happens very rapidly, and therefore you must repeat, review, recite, and review again almost up to the last minute in order not to let the memorized material become displaced or lost.

The only difference between calling studying "memorizing" or "cramming" is when it takes place. Memorizing is the rote repetition, review, and reciting we do whenever we try to learn something we need to retain. Cramming is the rote repetition, review, and reciting we do just before an exam in order to keep information fresh in our minds.

Research has shown that forgetting takes place faster while you are awake and slower while you are sleeping. If material is crammed just before going to sleep, it will be remembered longer than material learned before other activities. So if you have spent several days preparing for an exam and friends suggest a movie the night before it, saying "you deserve a break" or "it's too late to study now," don't listen! The night before the exam is the best time to study (especially if you have been preparing). So cram and then go right to bed and get a good night's sleep. And the next morning, try to find time to cram some more and to read over your answers to the predicted test questions right up to exam time.

Chapter Summary

To study for any kind of test, you need to start several days in advance. Collect and organize all your materials—class notes, textbooks, outside reading, and class assignments. Make study notes on the material topic by topic. Then condense those notes as tightly as you can and memorize them. Review and recite the information until you know it thoroughly. Cram the night before the exam, but get a good night's sleep, too. Cram some more the next morning before leaving to take the test. And then review, recite, and cram right up to exam time. Don't give yourself the opportunity to begin forgetting!

Chapter 4

Preparing for Essay Tests

Instructors give essay tests because they want to make an in-depth assessment of your knowledge of the course content. An essay exam measures higher levels of your understanding of the content than does an objective exam. By using good essay questions, the instructor can tell how well you can analyze, evaluate, and apply the concepts, ideas, and information presented in the course.

In addition to using the study techniques described in Chapter 3, you need to be able to predict the questions on the test and to practice writing essay answers to them. To predict the questions, you can use the test analysis form from Chapter 2. To practice the answers, you can use your organized study notes, which you learned how to make in Chapter 3. The questions you predict and the answers they require will help you decide what information to memorize and review. Reading through this chapter and working the exercises in it will give you experience in predicting short- and long-answer essay questions and in practicing how to answer them.

Predicting Questions

The easiest way to predict questions is if the instructor tells you what will be on the test. If that is not the case, turn to your test analysis form as well as your class notes and reading assignments and make a list of the topics that have been emphasized. Then develop them into essay questions. Even if your predicted questions don't turn out to be exactly like those on the exam, by developing your own questions, you have been actively thinking about and learning the material.

It sometimes helps to work on predicting questions with a friend taking the same course. You can each go through your own notes and predict questions. Your friend may have picked up some important notes or areas of emphasis that you missed. You also may be able to reach a greater understanding about a concept or a theory by discussing your notes and predicting questions together. A word of caution, however: Many students have problems with concentration when studying with others. Limit the joint study to predicting questions together. If you feel that even this distracts you, work alone next time.

There are different kinds of essay questions requiring somewhat different kinds of answers. In the pages that follow, you will learn how to fit these various kinds of questions to the kinds of information that have been presented in your course.

Short-Answer Questions

If your notes are *a list of people or things*, you can probably predict a short-answer question. Usually this kind of question requires only a couple of sentences or a paragraph at the most. Words like *list*, *name*, *define*, and *identify* are used by instructors when they ask a short-answer question.

To get an idea of how notes are used to predict short-answer questions, read over the following two sets of notes and the predicted short-answer question for each.

Notes:

U. S. Government
1) Executive branch
a. The President
B. Executive departments
C. Independent agencies
2) Legislative branch
a. Senate
B. House of Representatives
3) Judicial branch
a. Supreme Court
B. Other federal courts

Predicted Short-Answer Question:

List the three branches of the U. S. government and identify what those branches include.

Notes:

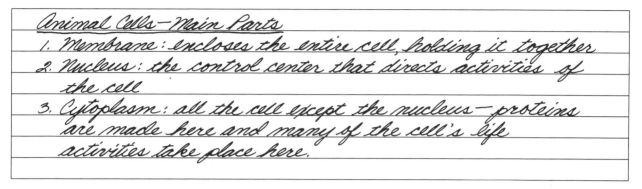

Animal Cells—Main Parts
1. *Membrane: encloses the entire cell, holding it together*
2. *Nucleus: the control center that directs activities of the cell*
3. *Cytoplasm: all the cell except the nucleus—proteins are made here and many of the cell's life activities take place here.*

Predicted Short-Answer Question:

List the three main parts of the animal cell and define them.

Exercise 4.1

Go through the two following sets of notes and predict a short-answer question for each, using words such as *list, name, define,* and *identify.* (Compare your answers with those in the back of the book.)

1. Notes:

Margaret Mitchell's "Gone with the Wind": Main Characters and Their Traits

Scarlett: vivacious, strong, optimistic, beautiful, life-force of her family, primary character of novel.
Ashley: dreamer, weak, ineffective, secondary male character, can't deal with the new life.
Rhett: strong, handsome, devilish personality, realist, primary male character, opportunist.
Melanie: gentle, represents goodness and decency, weak health, devotion and sweetness, secondary female character.

Predicted Short-Answer Question:

2. Notes:

> *Late-19th-Century American Authors*
>
> 1. Samuel Clemens (Mark Twain): "Tom Sawyer," "Huckleberry Finn," "A Connecticut Yankee in King Arthur's Court"
> 2. Edith Wharton: "Ethan Frome," "The Age of Innocence," "The House of Mirth"
> 3. Henry James: "Daisy Miller," "Portrait of a Lady," "The Bostonians"

Predicted Short-Answer Question:

_____

_____

Long-Answer "Trace" Questions

If your notes outline or describe *steps of a process or the historical development* of something, you can probably predict a "trace" question. Sometimes charts in textbooks or on handouts are also potential material for trace questions. Any of the following phrases signal a trace question.

- Describe the steps in . . .
- Trace the development of . . .
- Trace the events leading up to . . .
- Outline the history of . . .

Look through the two following sets of notes and see how the trace questions were predicted for them.

Notes:

> *How RNA Is Formed*
>
> 1. When RNA copies DNA's blueprint for making a protein, the DNA ladder first splits lengthwise through its bases—half serves as a mold to form the messenger, RNA.
> 2. Free RNA bases with attached sugars and phosphates match up with exposed DNA bases.
> 3. It forms as the reverse of the DNA blueprint and peels off the DNA mold.
> 4. Halves of DNA start to rejoin.
> 5. Completed RNA strand leaves nucleus and goes to the ribosomes.

Predicted Trace Question:

Describe the steps in the formation of RNA.

Notes:

Important Events Prior to the Revolutionary War

1763 — *Britain stationed a standing army in America and prohibited colonists from settling west of the Appalachian Mts.*

1765 — *Parliament passed the Stamp Act, taxing newspapers and legal documents in colonies.*

1770 — *British troops killed American civilians in Boston Massacre.*

1773 — *Colonists staged Boston Tea Party.*

1774 — *The Intolerable Acts closed Boston Harbor to punish colonists.*

Predicted Trace Question:

Trace the important events leading up to the Revolutionary War in America.

Exercise 4.2

Go through the following two sets of notes and predict a trace question for each, using one of the phrases listed above. (Compare your answers to those in the back of the book.)

1. Notes:

Distribution of Product from Manufacturer

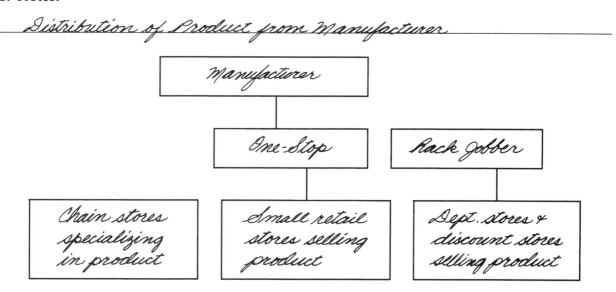

Predicted Trace Question:

_____

_____

2. Notes:

Events Leading to Great Depression

1. Dust storms in Midwest caused hardship to farmers
   during the 1920s.
2. The stock market crashed in 1929.
3. Frightened stockholders sold out.
4. Banks collapsed and businesses folded.
5. People lost their jobs, their savings, and their homes.

Predicted Trace Question:

_____

_____

Long-Answer "Compare and Contrast" Questions

If your notes describe _two or more things that have some similar and some dissimilar characteristics,_ you can usually predict a "compare and contrast" question. The following phrases usually signal a compare-and-contrast question.

- Tell how [two or more things] are alike or different.
- Weigh [or consider] the advantages or disadvantages of . . .
- Compare and contrast [two or more things].
- Show the similarities and differences between _____ and
  _____ .

Look through the two following sets of notes and see how the compare-and-contrast questions were predicted.

Notes:

Abe Lincoln – 1860s	John Kennedy – 1960s
Rights of citizenship for blacks	Equal rights for blacks
Assassinated in office	Assassinated in office
First Republican President	Democratic President
More interested in national affairs	Interested in both national and internat'l affairs
Self-educated, "plain folks," and poor	Highly educated, socially prominent, and wealthy
American hero	Became an American hero

Predicted Compare-and-Contrast Question:

Compare and contrast Presidents Lincoln and Kennedy.

Notes:

Psychologist	Psychiatrist
1. usually has M.A. or Ph.D. degree with special training in psychology	1. has M.D. degree and special training in mental illness
2. deals with animal & human behavior – normal & abnormal	2. deals with abnormal human behavior
3. does not prescribe medication	3. can prescribe medication

Predicted Compare-and-Contrast Question:

Show the similarities and differences between the work and training of the psychologist and the psychiatrist.

Exercise 4.3

Go through the two following sets of notes and predict a compare-and-contrast question for each, using the phrases listed above. (Compare your answers with those in the back of the book.)

1. Notes:

Ken Kesey's "One Flew Over the Cuckoo's Nest" — Main Characters and Their Traits

1. Randle McMurphy
   (institutionalized)

   boisterous
   rebel
   fun-loving
   strong-willed
   not insane
   feigns insanity for a
      softer life

2. Nurse Ratched
   (runs institution)

   calm
   authoritarian
   disciplinarian
   tyrant
   insane with power
   feigns sanity

3. Chief
   (institutionalized)

   silent
   passive
   strong
   huge
   probably not insane
   feigns being insane
      and deaf and dumb
      to escape the
      cruelties of life

Predicted Compare-and-Contrast Question:

_____

_____

2. Notes:

Great 20th-Century American Artists

Georgia O'Keeffe (from New Mexico): painter of organic abstract forms in strong, clear colors; frequently employed Southwest motifs, as in *Cow's Skull, Red, White, and Blue* (1931).

Louis Comfort Tiffany (from New York City): creator of new art form — used freely shaped iridescent glass combined with metal; designer of jewelry and buildings, painter, decorator, glassmaker, and philanthropist; part of Art Nouveau movement (1890-1910, swept thru Europe & America).

Frank Lloyd Wright (from Midwest): architect — designed more than 600 bldgs., including skyscrapers, factories, and private homes; main principle was "organic architecture" (bldg. should suit its inhabitants & surroundings).

Predicted Compare-and-Contrast Question:

_____

_____

Long-Answer "Discuss" Questions

If your notes describe *a specific individual, situation, or institution,* you can usually expect a "discuss" question. The following phrases signal a discuss question.

- Discuss the significance or the problems of . . .
- What is the relationship between _____ and _____ ?
- Discuss the effect of . . .
- Discuss the role of . . .

Look through the two following sets of notes and see how the discussion questions were predicted for each of them.

Notes:

Effects of the Civil War

1. Economy of South was crippled.
2. Republican Party gained control.
3. Heritage of hate was left on both sides.
4. Southern way of life ended.
5. Gov't created more jobs during Reconstruction.
6. Reconstruction period led to America's Industrial Era.

Predicted Discussion Question:

Discuss some of the effects of the Civil War in America.

Notes:

Franchising

Parent company sells others the right to open similar business under its name and supplies market identification and know-how — makes big profits.

Franchisee pays a fee to parent company, buys supplies from franchiser, and increases the value of the parent company through reputation of each franchise — franchisee's profits relatively smaller. Parent company runs risks because of big investments of money and chance of a franchise getting a bad image.

Predicted Discussion Question:

What is the relationship between the parent company and the franchiser?

Exercise 4.4

Go through the two following sets of notes and predict a discussion question for each, using the phrases listed above. (Compare your answers with those in the back of the book.)

1. Notes:

> _Hiroshima After the Bomb (1945)_
>
> 1. Approx. 350,000-400,000 people were vaporized by the searing heat in Hiroshima.
> 2. Approx. the same number ↑ died a short time after, in terrible pain.
> 3. (a) A third group lived but suffered wounds, burns, mental anguish, and massive doses of radiation (weak, sick to stomachs, loss of hair, change of cell structure causing cancer, genetic defects in children).
> (b) Many of these survivors fled Hiroshima after bombing and went to Nagasaki (200 mi. SW) and were killed in a second atomic-bomb blast.

Predicted Discussion Question:

_____

_____

2. Notes:

> _Jim Crow Laws (in segregationist and civil rights movements)_
> In 1828, Thomas Dartmouth Rice appeared on stage during a minstrel show with blackened face, old clothes, and sang song ident. himself as "Jim Crow." Characterization became a popular stereotype of the black man among racist whites. Whites saw in Jim Crow a black man who had the status they thought he deserved in a white society. Laws were passed after Civil War in the South to try to keep blacks "in their place," or segregated from whites. These laws became known as Jim Crow laws. Groups like the Ku Klux Klan enforced them. Laws stemming from these were the grandfather clause and the poll tax (prohibited voting rights). The attitudes expressed by Jim Crow laws proved to be more difficult to eradicate than the laws themselves.

Predicted Discussion Question:

_____

_____

Practicing Answers

Once you have looked over your test analysis form, organized your notes, and predicted the probable essay questions, you should practice answering them, using your notes. Following are some tips for answering essay questions.

1. Start off by turning the question into a statement.
2. Be sure that each point or idea is clearly stated and that they do not run together. It is helpful to outline your answer first.
3. Because neatness and organization can affect how many points your instructor will allow for your answers, it is a good idea to practice writing them with care so that organization and clear handwriting will come more naturally when you take the test. If you are not sure that your handwriting can be clearly read, ask a friend or family member to look over your answers and give you their opinion. Some students will gain by printing their answers.

Think of the predicted questions and practice answers as a dress rehearsal for your test. Save your practice answers to read over just before the test so they will be fresh in your memory.

Before you practice writing essay answers, read this example using the three points listed above.

Predicted Question:

Name the main characters in "Gone with the Wind" and give their traits.

Answer:

The main characters of "Gone with the Wind" are Scarlett, Rhett, Ashley, and Melanie. Scarlett, the primary character of the novel, is vivacious, strong, optimistic, beautiful, and the life-force of her family. Rhett, the primary male character, is strong and handsome with a devilish personality. Rhett is a realist and opportunist. Ashley, *the secondary male character, is a dreamer. He proves to be weak and ineffective and can't deal with the new life he's forced to live. Melanie, the secondary female character, is gentle, devoted, and sweet. Her health is weak. Melanie represents goodness and decency.*

Exercise 4.5

Practice writing essay answers to some of the questions you predicted earlier in the chapter.

1. *Late-19th-Century American Authors* (page 60)
   Predicted Question:

   _____

   _____

   Answer:

   _____

   _____

   _____

   _____

   _____

   _____

   _____

   _____

   _____

   _____

   _____

   _____

2. *Distribution of Product from Manufacturer* (page 62)
   Predicted Question:

   _____

   _____

   Answer:

   _____

   _____

   _____

   _____

   _____

   _____

   _____

   _____

   _____

   _____

   _____

   _____

3. *Great 20th-Century American Artists* (page 65)
   Predicted Question:

   _____

   _____

   Answer:

   _____

   _____

   _____

   _____

   _____

_____
_____
_____
_____
_____
_____

4. *Hiroshima After the Bomb* (page 67)
   Predicted Question:

_____
_____

   Answer:

_____
_____
_____
_____
_____
_____
_____
_____
_____
_____
_____
_____
_____
_____
_____

Improving Your Answers with Library Research

You can add to your study notes with citations, statistics, and other information from authorities on a particular topic by using the reference resources of the library. If your instructor suggested that you do outside reading or research on a topic, you can show that by citing references or pieces of information from that extra work on your essay test. Citing the name of one or two authorities and their articles can be enough to let your instructor know you have made a special effort to study. It is even better, however, to skim the articles at the library and take down a few important names and facts to use in your essay answers. Group this information with your other study notes on the topic.

The library has guides to various types of periodical literature, books, newspapers, documents, and surveys that can be used to identify the most current authors, articles, and statistics on all kinds of topics. To practice researching a topic or a famous person, follow these steps at your school library.

Researching a Topic.   Choose a topic to research.

Write it here. _____

1. Look up the topic and the person in *The Readers' Guide to Periodical Literature*, the most general library index, or ask the librarian which index would be most appropriate. Also ask the librarian for the appropriate descriptors if you have trouble finding your topic. List three sources on your subject.

Name of Periodical	Name of Article	Author	Date	Vol.	Pages
(1)					
(2)					
(3)					

2. Find one of the articles listed above and skim through it for two or three important facts (for example, the date of an important discovery or event, the name of an important person and his or her contribution, an important idea or concept, and the name of the responsible person).

(1) _____

_____

(2) _____

(3) _____

_____

3. Use the current *Statistical Abstract of the United States*. (This is published once a year by the U.S. Department of Commerce, Bureau of the Census; it is a national data book citing the most current statistics on a comprehensive range of trends, subjects, and topics.) Look up your topic in the index or table of contents of the *Statistical Abstract*. (Consult your librarian for relevant descriptors if you have trouble finding your topic.) Cite three statistics relevant to your topic and list the sources for those statistics.

Statistic	Source, or Survey Done by	Date
(1) _____		
(2) _____		
(3) _____		

Researching a Famous Person.   Choose a famous person to research.

Write his or her name here. _____

1. Use the *Biography Index* to find sources if the person you chose is no longer living. If the person is still alive, use the *Current Biography Index*. Find three sources (articles or books) in one of these indexes and provide the information below.

Source (name of book or periodical and article)	Author	Date	Pages
(1) _____			
(2) _____			
(3) _____			

2. Find one of the sources listed above and skim through it for two or three important facts about the person.

(1) _____

_____

(2) _____

_____

(3) _____

Exercise 4.6

Practice answering an essay question using both your study notes and notes from library research. Below are some sociology notes on mobility trends and causes. Following the notes are some library citations and statistics marked with an (*). Answer the predicted question using all the notes and the library citations.

Notes:

Causes of Current Mobility Trends in Urban U.S.

1. change of life style—caused by divorce, inflation, need for self-fulfillment

2. change of economic base—caused by divorce, job change, education, transfers in jobs (many businesses are moving away from metro areas because of inflation.)

3. rising inflation—affecting transportation (high cost of cars, gas) and desire for public transportation (more economical); cost of housing (housing closer to metro areas is often more costly, and housing further out— even outside suburbs—is often more reasonable.)

4. back-to-nature movement (move to country) and back-to-culture movement (move closer to metro life and advantages of big city—restore slum and old areas and live there)

   * Between 1950 and 1960, 1.1% of overall population moved into the central city.

   * Between 1950 and 1960, 3.8% of overall population moved outside the central city.

   * Between 1960 and 1970, 0.6% of overall population moved into the central city.

   * Between 1960 and 1970, 2.4% of overall population moved outside central city.

   * 1970-1978, 0.6% moved into central city.

   * 1970-1978, 1.5% moved outside central city.

   (Statistics from U.S. Bureau of the Census, *Census of Population* and *Current Population Reports*.)

Predicted Question:

Discuss the causes of the current mobility trends in the urban United States.

Outline:

Answer:

_____

_____

_____

_____

_____

_____

_____

_____

Chapter Summary

To prepare for an essay test, you must not only organize your notes and condense and memorize them, as you learned how to do in Chapter 3, but you must also predict the questions and practice answering them. From your notes, you can usually predict what kind of question you will be asked: short-answer questions (list, define, identify) or long-answer questions (trace, compare and contrast, discuss). You can add source citations and facts from library research about test topics to improve your score. Even if the questions you predict are not exactly the same as those on the test, the process of predicting questions and practicing answers will help you get to know the material thoroughly—it will make you a testwise student.

Chapter 5

Preparing for Objective Tests

While essay tests require some subjective judgment by the grader, there is only one correct way to answer multiple-choice, matching, true-false, and completion questions. The answers are marked right or wrong according to an answer key, and no matter who corrects the test, the results will be the same. Because correcting objective tests is simpler and less time-consuming than correcting essay tests, instructors are especially likely to use objective tests for large classes.

Taking an objective test (except for completion questions and some true-false questions) requires recognizing the right answer rather than recalling it from your memory bank. As noted in Chapter 3, recognition is easier than recall. Consequently, you can generally get by with a less thorough knowledge of a subject than is needed for essay tests. People who are already familiar with a topic can even sometimes pass an objective test about it without studying. Most of the time, however, you will need to gain familiarity with a topic by studying the course content. And remember, research shows that students who prepare for objective tests as thoroughly as they do for essay tests score higher than do students who have prepared only enough to recognize the right answers.

Studying for an objective test requires following the steps in Chapter 3: organize your class notes and readings, make study notes on each topic, condense those notes, memorize them, and review them over and over. In addition, you should also try to predict questions on the test, using your notes and test analysis form. To prepare for an objective test, you will spend less time practicing answers than is needed for an essay test; when you make up an objective question, you already know exactly what the answer should be. You may find it helpful, however, to spend some study time with a group and practice answering each other's predicted questions.

In this chapter, you will learn how to make multiple-choice, matching, true-false, and completion questions from your study notes. Even though you are not likely to predict the exact questions on your test, you will easily gain familiarity with the material through this process of predicting questions from your study notes.

Practicing Multiple-Choice Questions

To answer a multiple-choice question, you have to choose one of three, four, or five possible answers. The questions consist of a stem (also called a lead or an introduction) followed by the possible answers (also called alternatives). All the alternatives may be so different that the right choice is obvious, or they may be quite similar and require more careful consideration.

To see how study notes can be turned into multiple-choice questions, read through the following study notes and the two mutiple-choice questions predicted from those notes.

Notes:

> John Steinbeck's "The Grapes of Wrath"
>
> First published in 1939 — America was still getting over the Great Depression
> A powerful dramatization of the forced migration of people from their bank-foreclosed farms in the Dust Bowl
> A dramatization of the plight of the dispossessed everywhere
> A great social document of an era in American history
> Main characters were the Joad family — "Okie" farmers

Predicted Multiple-Choice Questions:

> 1. Which one of the following statements is not true about "The Grapes of Wrath"?
> A. It portrays the plight of the dispossessed.
> B. It is a great social document dramatizing the forced migration of people.
> C. It takes place during World War II in the United States.
> D. The main characters were a family of "Okie" farmers.

2. "The Grapes of Wrath" is a book about:

A. the Goad family, who owned a vineyard in California during the Great Depression.

B. the Sartoris family, who moved from Oklahoma to California during the Great Depression.

C. the Goad family, who moved from the Dust Bowl to California during World War II.

D. the Goad family, whose plight represents that of the dispossessed everywhere.

Answers: _1, C; 2, D_

Exericse 5.1

Using the sample class notes from Chapter 4 about RNA and about the Great Depression, predict a multiple-choice question on each topic.

Predicted Multiple-Choice Question based on "How RNA Is Formed" (page 60):

(Stem) _____

_____

A. _____

B. _____

C. _____

D. _____

Answer: _____

Predicted Multiple-Choice Question based on "Events Leading to Great Depresssion" (page 62):

(Stem) _____

A. _____

_____

B. _____

_____

C. _____

_____

D. _____

_____

Answer: _____

Practicing Matching Questions

Matching questions are easy to make up because you do not need to think up alternatives to the right answer. You simply make a list of stems, or leads, and a list of correct answers to complete them—in a different order. To make a matching question harder, you can add more possible answers in the second column than there are stems in the first.

To see how a matching question is made from study notes, read through the following notes on the novels *Babbitt* and *The Big Money* and the predicted matching question based on them and the notes from *The Grapes of Wrath* (page 78).

Notes:

"*Babbitt*" by Sinclair Lewis

Published in 1922

Babbitt, a conniving and prosperous real estate man is the main character

Portrays total conformist

Aspires for power in his community and self-esteem

Is so filled with rationalizations that he doesn't recognize his own corruption

A hardened and professional social climber

"The Big Money" by John Dos Passos
Published in 1937
One of the trilogy, "U.S.A.," which also includes "The
    42nd Parallel" and "1919"
The classic novel of the "lost generation" of the 1920s
The "lost generation" includes actresses, aviators, flappers, the
    Fords, social workers and is characterized by money-
    making, murder, speakeasies, dreams, and delusions
Main characters are: Charley Anderson—simple aviator hero
                     Mary French—who loved humanity
                     Marge Dowling—became the nation's
                                   sweetheart on the
                                   silver screen
                     Dick Savage—public relations expert
                                 who climbed to power and
                                 self-destruction

Predicted Matching Question:

Match the information with the appropriate novel. More than one of
the descriptions in column two may apply to a novel.

1. "The Grapes of Wrath"   A. Classic novel of "lost generation" of 1920s

2. "Babbitt"   B. Portrays the total conformist

3. "The Big Money"   C. Portrays the plight of the
                                     dispossessed

                                  D. Main characters are poor farmers

                                  E. Main characters are actress, aviator,
                                     money-maker, social worker

                                  F. Main character is a corrupt
                                     social climber

Answer: 1: C, D; 2: B, F; 3: A, E

Exercise 5.2

Using the sample class notes from Chapter 4 about the U.S. government and about *One Flew Over the Cuckoo's Nest,* predict a matching question for each topic.

Predicted Matching Question based on "U.S. Government" (page 58):

_____   _____

_____   _____

_____   _____

_____   _____

_____   _____

_____   _____

_____   _____

_____   _____

Answer: _____

Predicted Matching Question based on "Ken Kesey's *One Flew Over the Cuckoo's Nest*—Main Characters and Their Traits" (page 64):

_____   _____

_____   _____

_____   _____

_____   _____

_____   _____

_____   _____

_____   _____

Answer: _____

Practicing True-False Questions

True-false questions (which can also be yes-no or right-wrong) test your knowledge of the material and your ability to read carefully and critically. Some statements are obviously true or obviously false. But a statement can also be mixed; that is, part of it may be true and part of it false—which means you would mark the entire statement false. True-false questions can also be made more difficult by asking for an explanation of why a statement is false; this explanation may be written out or the word or phrase that makes the statement false may be underlined.

As examples of true-false questions made from study notes, here are two based on the notes from *The Grapes of Wrath* (page 78).

Predicted True-False Questions:

1. "The Grapes of Wrath" was first published long after the Great Depression. True or False?

2. In "The Grapes of Wrath," the Goad family moved to the Dust Bowl. True or False? If false, explain why.

Answers: 1, false; 2, false, because the Goad family moved from the Dust Bowl to California.

Exercise 5.3

Using the sample class notes from Chapter 4 about cell structure and about franchising, predict a true-false question for each topic.

Predicted True-False Question based on "Animal Cells—Main Parts" (page 59):

_____

_____

Answer: _____

Predicted True-False Question based on "Franchising" (page 66):

_____

_____

Answer: _____

Practicing Completion Questions

Completion, or fill-in-the-blank, questions are the most difficult objective questions because they require free-association answers. That is, you must fill in the blank by recalling information in your memory bank; there are usually no alternatives to choose from (there is a simpler kind of completion question that asks you to fill in the blank from a list of alternatives, which makes it essentially a multiple-choice question—but this kind of completion question is more common in the elementary grades than in high school or college). To answer completion questions, you may need to memorize entire definitions, theorems, laws, or passages.

Even though completion questions are the hardest kind of objective questions to answer, they are probably the easiest to construct. Here are two examples of predicted completion questions based on the notes from *The Big Money* (page 81).

Predicted Completion Questions:

1. "The Big Money" is the classic novel of
   of the 1920s.
2. _____ is the aviator hero in
   "The Big Money."

Answers: 1, the "lost generation"; 2, Charley Anderson

Exercise 5.4

Using the sample class notes from Chapter 4 about the American Revolution and about Jim Crow laws, predict a completion question for each topic.

Predicted Completion Question based on "Important Events Prior to the Revolutionary War" (page 61):

_____

_____

Answer: _____

Predicted Completion Question based on "Jim Crow Laws" (page 67):

_____

_____

Answer: _____

Group Study for Objective Tests

Since it is no challenge to answer the objective questions you have made from your study notes, it can be helpful to study with a group and test each other with your predicted questions. By taking someone else's predicted test, you can practice answering objective questions and identify information that you need to review some more by yourself (using the techniques in Chapter 4).

Although group study can be an excellent way to prepare for an objective test, research shows that students who study in groups tend to get lower scores on tests than students who study on their own. This is probably because group study is often not organized, concentration can be difficult, and study time can too easily become "party time." Here are some pointers to help you get the most out of group study for an objective test (but remember, you should not devote your entire study time to group study).

1. Carefully select group members; they should be people who are well prepared and not likely to try to distract the group.
2. Agree before your study session to each prepare a set of predicted questions based on your study notes; it might be a good idea to decide how many kinds of questions you each will do, too.
3. At your study session, exchange the tests you have each written, so everyone has a copy of all the tests done by everyone else in the group.
4. Take the practice tests one at a time and have the writer of one test read the correct answers before going on to the next test. If there are questions about any answers, discuss them before going on to another test. You may find it necessary to refer to your study notes to verify a disputed answer.

Standardized Tests

There is a category of objective tests that assesses your general knowledge of certain topics rather than your specific knowledge of the content of a course. You will undoubtedly encounter a number of these standardized tests during your years as a student—whether it's the GED (high school equivalency exam), the SAT (scholastic aptitude test), or one of the many kinds of exams required to qualify for entry into graduate school (or a profession) in a particular field.

There are two major kinds of standardized tests: norm-referenced tests and criterion-referenced tests. The primary difference between the two is how the test results are reported. For a norm-referenced test, the examinee's score is expressed as a comparison with how others have scored on the same test (a 50-percent score means that half the test-takers scored higher and half lower). For a criterion-referenced test, the examinee's score expresses how successfully he or she met the objectives from which the test was developed (a 50-percent score means that half the questions were answered correctly.)

The preparation for both kinds of standardized tests is the same. Be as well read in the subject as possible; there may be study guides available at your bookstore for the test you will be taking, or the test developer may furnish objectives or a description of the test content. Use the test-taking cues described in Chapter 8, but remember that the more familiar you are with the subject matter, the better chance you will have of eliminating the incorrect alternatives in the multiple-choice questions that are the most common kind of objective questions in standardized tests.

Chapter Summary

Predicting questions for objective tests is a useful way to gain familiarity with the material. If you know the test will have multiple-choice, matching, true-false, or fill-in-the-blank questions, make up those types of questions from your notes. Extensive review of your notes (using the study techniques from Chapter 3) and anticipating questions indicated as test topics and information on your test analysis form is the logical way to study for an objective exam. It can be helpful to spend some of your study time exchanging and taking practice exams with a small group of other students in your class.

Part Three

Taking Tests

Chapter 6

Getting Organized to Take the Test

This is it! The day of the exam! This is when all your preparation will pay off. Use the following steps to ensure that you will be as organized as possible for the test.

On Your Way

1. *Gather all the necessary materials.* Before leaving for the test, be sure you have your condensed notes, pens, sharpened pencils with erasers, plenty of clean paper, and a wristwatch. Allow enough time to get all of these items together. If your instructor prefers a certain type of paper or exam booklet or a certain color of pencil or ink, have the right kind ready. Also, take along any special instruments you will need, such as a ruler or a calculator.

2. *Wear comfortable clothes and shoes.* You want to be relaxed and able to concentrate your full attention on the test.

3. *Psych yourself up for the test.* Review your reasons from Chapter 1 for doing well on it.

4. *Leave a little early* so you'll have about fifteen minutes after you arrive at the test room before the test starts. If you have to rush to get to the test, you'll make yourself unnecessarily anxious.

5. When you arrive at the test room, find a quiet place before going in to *review and recite any notes* that had to be memorized verbatim. Then put your notes away and do not take them out again until after you have finished the test.

In the Test Room

6. Walk into the test room about five or ten minutes early and *find a seat where you will be comfortable* (if seats are not already assigned). Some students prefer sitting in the back row; others, in the front. Whatever your preference, sit where you will have plenty of elbow room and no one close enough to distract you during the test.

7. While waiting for the exam to be given out, *get your pens, pencils, and other materials out and ready.* Organize them on the top of your desk.

8. If you are becoming anxious, *practice some of the relaxation techniques* from Chapter 1.

Before Starting to Answer

9. Your instructor will give out the tests and direct you to write the answers on the test, your own paper, or an answer sheet or exam booklet. *Listen carefully to all directions* from your instructor. If you are confused about any of them, immediately raise your hand and ask for clarification.

10. *Write your name and other required identifying information* on the test or the answer sheet. Do not waste time supplying unnecessary information. For example, some instructors use machine-scorable answer sheets for objective exams that often have blanks for age, date of birth, name of school, and so on. If your instructor asks you to furnish only your name and the date, then ignore the other blanks.

11. *Jot down memorized facts.* As soon as the instructor has given directions and the test has officially begun, write down all the names, dates, formulas, or theorems you reviewed just before entering the test room—as well as any other facts from your study notes that come to mind immediately. This will take a minute or two of test time but will be well worth it because you will not risk forgetting these facts while you look over the test. And you will have them at hand when you need them to answer a question. Do not begin to jot these facts down until the exam has officially started, however; you do not want there to be any question about the possibility of cheating.

12. *Position the exam so you won't have to cross your arm over your line of vision to record each answer.* If you are right-handed, put the exam on the left side of the desk and the answer sheet on the right. If you are left-handed, put the exam on the right side of the desk and the answer sheet on the left.

13. *Assess the exam.* Quickly look it over from beginning to end to get a sense of the number and type of questions and their point values.

14. *Make a schedule for completing the test.* Because you want to give yourself the chance to answer all the questions that you know the answers to, you need to pace yourself. If you spend too much time on a difficult question, you might not have time left to answer easier ones that come after it. The kind of schedule you will make for an essay test is somewhat different from that for an objective test, and they will be explained in Chapters 7 and 8. But whichever kind of test you are taking, you will need to allow time to go through it a first time answering all the questions that are easy for you, to come back a second time to complete the more difficult questions, and to do a final check for careless errors and omissions.

15. If, at any time during the test, you find yourself tensing up, take a minute and *do some of the relaxation exercises* described in Chapter 1 so you will be able to concentrate on the test.

Chapter Summary

When you take a test, you want to be able to concentrate on turning the information you have been studying into the correct answers. There are a thousand little things that can distract you, but you can keep them to a minimum by being organized. Make sure you have all the necessary test-taking materials—from pencils to exam booklets—before you go to take the test. Give yourself ample time to get to the test room and to quickly review important memorized facts before going in to sit down.

If you can, find a seat where you will not be distracted by others taking the test and where you will have plenty of elbow room. When the test is handed out, listen carefully to the directions and immediately ask about any that are not clear. Jot down all the facts you've memorized for the test, and then make a game plan for taking the test to give yourself the opportunity to answer every question as well as you possibly can.

Chapter 7

Taking an Essay Test

Because essay questions require recall memory rather than just recognition, instructors use them to evaluate how *thoroughly* you have mastered course material. Consequently, essay questions require more from you. They require not only very thorough study but also the ability to provide answers that are complete, well organized, clear, and neat.

The form of your essays is also important because essay tests are graded more subjectively than objective tests; there is not just one simple way to answer each question. Although most instructors have an answer key that lists the concepts and facts they think the ideal answers should contain, your grade depends on your ability to communicate those concepts and facts to your instructor. Incomplete essays, ones that weave back and forth from point to point, ones that don't directly answer the question, or ones that are hard to read give the instructor the impression that the student doesn't know the material.

If you've studied according to the procedure described in Chapters 3 and 4, you should know the material thoroughly. In this chapter, you will learn how to communicate that knowledge on an essay test. Your goal is to answer all the questions as thoroughly, clearly, and concisely as possible. To do that, you need to budget your time; your essay needs to answer specifically the question that is asked; and your answer should be written neatly and in an organized manner.

Budget Your Time

After you have gotten the test and unloaded the facts from your memory, *quickly look over the exam* to see how many questions you will have to answer and how many points each is worth. For example, you may be asked to answer two out of three or one out of two from each section or three out of five from the entire test. You should note whether the questions in one section are worth more than the questions in another. If the test does not indicate the point value of the questions, immediately ask your instructor.

As you read through the test, you will notice that certain questions seem like they will be easier for you to answer than others. *Choose the questions now that you will answer.* As you read, concepts and facts to include in your answer may occur to you, so note them as you go through the test. These should be one- or two-word notes to jog your memory when you come back to write out the answers; don't try to compose the answer now.

After you have assessed how many questions you have to answer and how much each is worth, *plan a schedule.* You will want to allow time to read each question carefully, to outline the answers, and to make a final check for careless omissions and errors.

As an example, let's look at how you would budget your time to take an essay test in 55 minutes that has three equally weighted questions. You know you'll want at least 5 minutes to assess the test, choose your questions, and make your schedule. You know you'll want to spend the last 4 or 5 minutes of the test period doing a final check. And you want to allow yourself about 10 minutes before that to reread your answers and make sure they are complete or to finish any answer that still needs some work. Those three steps will use up 19 or 20 minutes, leaving you with 35 or 36 minutes to answer the questions. So, since you have three equally weighted questions, you should spend 12 minutes on each question—2 or 3 minutes on an outline and the remaining 9 or 10 minutes writing out the answer. If you made a diagram of your test-taking schedule, it would look something like this.

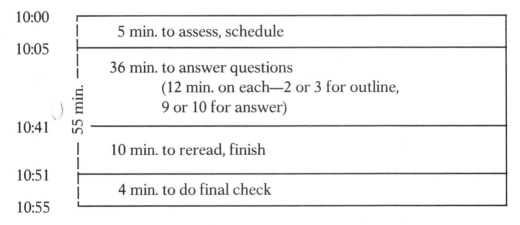

Sometimes the questions will not be equally weighted, however. If this is the case, you should adjust your schedule so you can spend more time on the question or questions that are worth more points. For example, if you had to answer three questions and one was worth twice as much as each of the other two, you should spend twice as much time on that question. Using the example above, you would spend 18 minutes to answer a more valuable question and 9 minutes each for the other two.

Read the Question Carefully

Your answer must fit the question. If the instructor asks you to analyze an event, a simple description of it will not do. If you are asked to interpret a poem, you should not just summarize it.

In Chapter 4, you learned that your notes can help you predict the kinds of essay questions you're likely to face: short-answer questions or long-answer trace, compare-and-contrast, or discussion questions. In this section, you'll learn some of the "exam words" that are used to signal those different types of questions and the appropriate kind of essay answer to write for each of them. First, you should read carefully through the words and their answer descriptions in the box "Essay Exam Terms." Then practice applying them by doing Exercise 7.1.

Essay Exam Terms

Short-Answer Terms

Classify.   Group the information in a diagram, chart, or description according to its main parts or characteristics.

Define.   Give concise, clear, and authoritative meaning. Don't give details, but make sure you have given a complete definition. Show how the thing you are defining differs from things in other classifications, if necessary.

Diagram.   Make a drawing, chart, plan, or other graphic answer. Label the information in it. It is a good idea to add a brief explanation or description.

Enumerate.   Write in a list or in an outline form. Give points concisely and one-by-one.

Give an Example.   Cite one instance or one situation to support or exemplify the general point.

Illustrate.   Use a picture, diagram, or concrete example to explain or clarify.

List.   Write an itemized series of concise statements giving names, things, or points one-by-one.

Name.   Make a list of all the important names or components.

State.   Present the main points in a brief, clear sequence, usually omitting details, illustrations, or examples.

Summarize.   Give the main points or facts in a condensed form, omitting small details and examples.

Long-Answer Trace Terms

Describe.   Recount or relate in sequence the steps requested. (Note: This can also be a short-answer signal if you are asked to describe a single thing rather than a sequence; then you would characterize or sketch the thing in expository form.)

Outline. Organize a description under main points and subordinate points, stressing the process or relationship among events. (Note: This can also be a short-answer signal if it is a single thing rather than a sequence to be outlined; in that case, omit minor details and use the outline to describe or classify.)

Trace. In narrative form, describe the process, development, steps, or historical events.

Long-Answer Compare-and-Contrast Terms

Compare. Emphasize the similarities between two (or more) things and, in some cases, also mention the differences.

Contrast. Stress the differences between objects, ideas, qualities, characteristics, events, or concepts.

Relate. Show how things are connected to each other or how one thing causes another, correlates with another, or is similar to another.

Long-Answer Discussion Terms

Analyze. Carefully appraise the situation or problem, citing both advantages and limitations. Emphasize your personal evaluation in light of the appraisal of authorities you have noted.

Criticize. Express your judgment about the merit or truth of the factors, concepts, or views mentioned. Give the results of your analysis of them, discussing their strong points and limitations.

Defend. Present one side of an argument, issue, or situation. If you can, cite the view of authorities or some data to support your side.

Discuss. Examine, analyze carefully, and give the reasons and all relevant details about a specific situation, individual, or institution. Be as complete and detailed as possible.

Evaluate. Carefully appraise the problem or situation, citing both advantages and limitations. Emphasize the appraisal of authorities and, to a lesser degree, your personal appraisal.

Explain. Interpret, clarify, and carefully spell out the material you present. Give reasons for differences of opinion or of results. Try to analyze the causes of the differences.

Interpret. Translate, give examples of, solve, or comment on a subject. Give your judgment about it in light of all you know about it.

Justify. Prove or give reasons for decisions or conclusions. Try hard to be convincing. Cite authorities or data to support your position.

Prove. Establish that something is true by citing factual evidence or giving a clear, logical reason.

Review. Examine a subject critically, analyzing and commenting on the important information about it.

Exercise 7.1

To check your knowledge of the meanings of the essay test terms, read each of the descriptions below and write in the blank the term the instructor should use in wording the essay question. In some cases, more than one word will fit the question. Compare your answers with those in the back of the book.

1. In the United States government course, the instructor wants the students to think over the functions and responsibilities of the Department of the Navy and the Department of the Army and to bring out the points of difference. Which term should be used in the question?

    _____

2. The instructor in an American history class mentions a body of water in the possession of the enemy in wartime. A plan is proposed for retaking it. If the students are to express their judgments on the merits of the plan, what term should be used in the question?

    _____

3. When and where did the American penal system have its beginning? What has been the general history of its development? The criminology instructor wants the students to follow the course of its progress. What term should be used?

    _____

4. Which term should a world history instructor use to ask for a concrete example of the use of submarines in World War II?

    _____

5. In an art course the instructor has discussed the experimental work of Cezanne, Van Gogh, and others. On a written examination the students are to pick out the main points of the discussion and bring them together in a concise overall statement. What term should be used in the question?

    _____

6. In a chemistry class the instructor wants the students to make clear the nature of a chemical-bond reaction. How does it come about? Which term should be used in the question?

    _____

7. In an economics class the instructor has lectured on the decontrol of oil and gas prices. On the test, the students will need to think over the topic and consider it from various points of view. They will be asked to present different sides of the issue. Which term should be used in the question?

_____

8. In an English course the instructor has assigned a term paper and has told the students how to proceed in collecting the data. On a quiz they will have to give the steps briefly one after another. Which term should be used?

_____

9. In a geology class, the instructor has used television to show how cross-bedding is a common feature of sandstones. On a quiz the instructor wants to be sure that the students really know the meaning of the term *cross-bedding*. What term should be used in the question?

_____

10. A literature instructor wants the students to consider the ways in which early French, Spanish, and English literature are alike and the ways in which they are different. What term should be used in the question?

_____

The key words in an essay question are not only the essay test terms but also the *subjects of the questions*. Are you being asked to trace the events leading up to the Revolutionary War or the main events of the war? Are you being asked to compare the works of a number of great American artists, or their lives? Take the time to read the question carefully.

Outline the Answer

If the essay question calls for a long or complex answer, you should outline it before you begin to write it out. The outline will help you organize your answer and include all the important concepts and facts. Because an outline will give order to your answer, you will find that writing it out will be easy; it will be a simple matter of turning the outline points into sentences.

When making an outline of your answer, think back to your notes. How was the material organized there? Also, which essay test terms are used in the question? What is its subject? Try to visualize your notes, readings, and lectures about the topic. What points were covered? What was emphasized? Your purpose is to try to cover all the main concepts and facts that the instructor will be looking for when grading the question.

An outline should be brief; use short phrases and abbreviations, and leave out the little connecting words. Don't spend a lot of time writing your outline; its purpose is to ensure order and completeness to your answer. Don't try to formulate your sentences in the outline. Spend just a few minutes on it and leave the better part of the time allotted in your schedule to writing out the answer. (If you need to review how to make an outline, refer to page 51 in Chapter 3.)

Keep all the key words in the exam question in mind so that your answer will fit the question. When you feel your outline is complete, look it over to make sure that it completely covers the important points and is logically organized. Be sure the information is in the order in which you will want it in the written-out answer. If you want to change the order of the main headings or subtopics, don't rewrite the entire outline. That will waste valuable time. Just renumber the main headings or subtopics.

When you make your outline, include the relevant facts that you memorized and jotted down just before starting the test. Look them over to see if any of them apply to the answer you have outlined. Insert any that do into the appropriate spot in the outline. Don't rewrite them there, though. Just identify them in some way (perhaps with asterisks or circled letters or numbers) and put the symbol in the appropriate spot in the outline so that when you are writing out your answer, you will know where to include the fact.

You should write your outline on some clean notebook paper separate from your answers or on the back pages of the exam booklet, if one is provided. *If you run out of time before you have had a chance to write out one of your answers, you can at least turn in the outline.* Although you probably won't get full credit for the answer, you will get some points for showing that you know what the important elements are.

If your time runs out and you must turn in an outline instead of an essay, be sure to indicate on the outline which question it is for and insert it in the proper order between the other essay answers. Then write a quick note at the top of the outline to let your instructor know that you ran out of time before you could put it in paragraph form. Ask the instructor to evaluate the outline as your answer to the question.

Write Out the Answer

Your goal is to write a compact, complete, organized, and clear essay in answer to each question. To know a little and present it well is better than knowing much but presenting it poorly. Your logical outline is a solid beginning.

The Opening Statement

Rephrase the question as an opening statement. This is the start to your answer. Once you have this opening statement before you, your thoughts will be more likely to flow. To practice writing opening statements, do Exercise 7.2.

Exercise 7.2

For each of the questions below, pick out the essay test terms and the subjects and then rewrite the question into an opening statement. Refer to the notes for each question on the indicated pages.

The first question has been done for you as an example. When you finish the others, compare your answers to those in the back of the book.

Example Question:

List the three branches of the U.S. government and identify what they include. (See notes on page 58.)

Exam Term(s): _list, identify_

Subject of Question: _three branches of U.S government_

Opening Statement: _The three branches of the U.S government are the executive, legislative, and judicial branches._

1. Question:

Identify three late-nineteenth-century American authors and their works. (See notes on page 60.)

Exam Term(s): _____

Subject of Question: _____

Opening Statement: _____

_____

2. Question:

Describe the steps in the formation of RNA. (See notes on page 60.)

Exam Term(s): _____

Subject of Question: _____

Opening Statement: _____

_____

3. Question:

Trace the events leading up to the Revolutionary War in America. (See notes on page 61.)

Exam Term(s): _____

Subject of Question: _____

Opening Statement: _____

_____

4. Question:

Compare and contrast the great American art forms and works of Georgia O'Keeffe, Louis Tiffany, and Frank Lloyd Wright. (See notes on page 65.)

Exam Term(s): _____

Subject of Question: _____

Opening Statement: _____

_____

5. Question:

Discuss some of the effects of the Civil War in America. (See notes on page 66.)

Exam Term(s): _____

Subject of Question: _____

Opening Statement: _____

_____

Essay Paragraphs

After you write the opening statement, refer to your outline and give the information in the first main heading, keeping the key words in the question in mind. Then complete the paragraph with the subtopics—which will probably be two to four details, examples, or pieces of supportive information—and include the relevant memorized facts.

Start the second paragraph to give information under the second main heading, and so on. When you have covered all the main headings in your outline, write one or two sentences to summarize your answer. A clear beginning and ending to your answer will make it seem well thought-out.

This pattern is a deductive one, where you go from the main idea to the specifics. If you were asked to give the details first and then arrive at the main idea, you would use inductive organization. In this case, you would work from the bottom of each main topic to the top—or from the specifics to the subtopics to the main idea.

As you write your answer, qualify specifics if you are not sure you remember them correctly. For example, it is better to say "toward the end of the eighteenth century" than "in 1793" if you're not sure if it was 1793 or 1783. Avoid definite numbers and dates that you're not completely sure of. Often, an approximation is all that is necessary.

After you have finished writing out your essay, leave sufficient space in case you decide to add some essential information that you discover you omitted.

Neatness

Your instructor will be favorably impressed by legible handwriting, ample margins, and separation of paragraphs by indentions. Research has shown that these elements of neatness are important variables in scoring. So when you write your answer, keep the following points in mind.

1. *Write your words so that they can be read* by others. If your handwriting is hard to read, you might print your answer.
2. *Try to use correct spelling, punctuation, and grammar.* Your instructor will be more impressed with your answer if you have used traditional spelling and grammar, and if your thoughts are clearly separated by appropriate punctuation.
3. When you start a new idea or a new paragraph, *indent* to separate it from the previous paragraph. This is a way to show your instructor how many ideas or examples you have been able to recall and discuss.
4. *Leave sufficient margins* along all four sides of the page. This makes the answer look neater. It also allows room for you to insert additional information that you realize at the last minute that you had left out.
5. *Erase or cross out carefully.* Don't leave your paper smudged and torn up from erasing. And don't make your instructor wonder what is and is not part of your answer. Also, make your changes and insertions clear and easy to follow.

Reread Your Answers

Once you have completed the essays for each question, reread each one. When writing in haste, it is easy to misspell words, to write illegibly, to miswrite dates and figures, and to omit words (or parts of words) and even parts of answers. As you go back over your essays, watch for these common errors. Also, check to see that you have used all the memorized facts that you could. If you need to add anything lengthy, use the space you left after your answer and draw an arrow from the additional information to the part of the answer to which it refers. These last-minute corrections and additions may add appreciably to your grade and generally improve the impression your paper will make on your instructor. But be sure to make them as neat as possible.

Make a Final Check

In the last few minutes before the testing session ends, make a final check. Be sure your name and any other necessary information (date, class name, section number) is on every page of your answers. Then gather your answers together and check the order of the pages. When you turn your test in, ask the instructor if you also need to turn in your scratch papers containing the outlines and the jotted-down facts. If so, indicate at the top of each page that they are "scratch sheets."

Chapter Summary

To take an essay test, you need to budget your time after assessing the number of questions and choosing the ones that seem the easiest for you to answer. You'll need to allow time to read the questions carefully, paying attention to the essay test terms and the subjects of the questions. Then, if the question calls for a long-answer essay, outline your answer so it will include all the important points from your study notes and the list of memorized facts you jotted down just before starting on the test.

When you write your answer from the outline, keep the following pattern in mind.

1. Write an *opening statement* that rephrases the question.
2. Develop the *main points* of your outline one paragraph at a time.
3. Follow the topic sentence (main point) of each paragraph with two to four *details, examples, or supportive citations*.
4. Write a one- or two-sentence *summary*.
5. Leave *room between each answer* in case you decide to add more after rereading it.

Finally, try to give yourself enough time to reread your answers and to make a final check—and if you run out of time before writing one of the essays, hand in your outline.

Chapter 8

Taking an Objective Test

Now that you have completed the steps listed in Chapter 6 for organizing yourself to take the test, you are ready to begin. Having studied thoroughly (as described in Chapters 3 and 5) will be your best insurance that you will do well. There are some special techniques for taking objective tests, however, that the testwise student must know as well.

First, you need to have a strategy for taking the test; turning the test in after you have gone through it once is not being testwise. In this chapter, you'll learn how to pace yourself so you'll have time to go through the test a second time and then make a final check before you turn it in. You'll become a testwise student who knows steps for taking an objective test.

Then you'll learn how to look for cues in the questions that will help you recognize the right answer. Some kinds of cues apply to several kinds of objective questions; other cues are specific to multiple-choice, matching, true-false, or completion questions. Finally, you'll learn when and how to guess on questions that you are not able to answer from your knowledge and your search for cues.

Test-Taking Steps

To give yourself the chance to answer correctly all the questions that you can, you need to budget your time (as was pointed out in Chapter 6). For an objective test, you'll want enough time to go through it three times. First, go through and answer all the questions you know, spending an equal amount of time on each one and not getting bogged down on difficult questions. (If some test sections are worth more than others, however, allow more time for the sections worth more points. If you can't tell how many points the sections or questions are worth, ask your instructor immediately.) The second time you go through the test, your goal is to try to answer the questions that you couldn't the first time (later in this chapter you'll find some cues to help you identify the right answer). The third time through, go back over your entire answer sheet and check for forgotten questions, stray marks, and misnumbered answers.

Budget Your Time

To figure out how to budget your time for a test, you first need to know how long the test session is. Subtract from that amount of time 5 minutes to read all the directions thoroughly, and to decide on your test-taking schedule. Subtract another 5 minutes for your final check. So if you had 55 minutes to take a test, you would subtract 10 from 55, leaving you 45 minutes for the first and second go-throughs.

To decide how much time you can spend on each question, you need to know how many questions are in the test, and then allot a little more time for the first go-through than for the second. For example, if your test had 50 objective questions worth two points each, you could spend half a minute on each question the first time through, which would total 25 minutes. That would leave you 20 minutes for the second go-through. If you made a diagram of your test-taking schedule, it would look something like this.

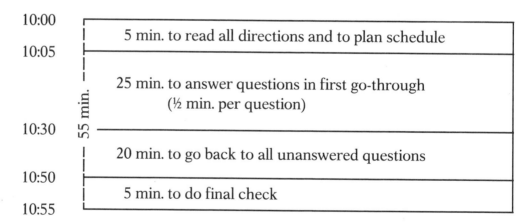

Read the Directions

Read all the directions carefully before you start to answer any questions. If there are directions for each section of the test, reread them before you begin to answer any questions in the section.

Read the directions critically; don't assume you already know what they say. For example, on a multiple-choice test, it is easy to assume that you are to select the best answer. The directions, however, might tell you to select the least appropriate answer. Or you might asssume that for true-false items, you are to indicate "T" or "F." But the directions might tell you to answer "yes" or "no," or to add or delete words from all false statements to make them true. Or you might assume that for matching questions you are to match the Column 2 items to the Column 1 items by writing the letter or number from Column 2 next to its match in Column 1. But the directions could tell you to draw a line from each item in Column 1 to its match in Column 2. In short, if you ignore the directions, you might not get credit for your answers even if you knew the material thoroughly.

Your First Go-Through

Now that you have read the directions carefully, and planned a schedule for taking the test, you are ready to begin answering questions. On this first go-through, you will answer the questions that are easy for you. But remember to read all the choices for each question before answering, even if you think you have spotted the right answer. (It is strongly recommended that you take an objective test in pencil!) Keep the following points in mind as you work your way through the test the first time.

- *Attempt every question, but answer only the easiest ones the first time through.* Remember that questions that look difficult and involved may turn out not to be. Work through the entire test item by item, no matter how hard some of them may appear; spend your allotted time on each question.

- *Read each question thoroughly and critically.* The difference between a right and a wrong answer can often be a single word.

- But *don't overinterpret questions.* The more time you spend laboring over a question—once you have read it carefully—the more likely you are to read something into it that's not there. Students sometimes think that the right answer is too obvious and that the instructor must be trying to trick them. Most instructors don't do this. The right answer may seem obvious simply because you know the material well.

- *Establish a system for going back to questions later.* This will help you with your second go-through. If you answer a question and then feel a little unsure about it, put a small pencil dot next to it. On a multiple-choice test, you might have narrowed down the answer to a couple of alternatives; mark them with a light pencil check so you can save time during the second go-through by ignoring the alternatives you're sure are wrong. For matching questions, you might lightly check the items still to be matched. For true-false and completion questions, you might lightly check the ones you think you have an answer for (there might be cues in later questions that could confirm the answer) and put a small dot next to those you have no idea about. Whatever the symbols, it is important to make some signposts for the second go-through.

Your Second Go-Through

As soon as you have gone through the last item on the test, you are ready to begin your second go-through. If you have been following your schedule, you should have time to go back to all the unanswered questions, starting with those at the beginning of the test.

Do not be concerned if other students finish the test before you do. They may be finishing faster because they know the material better, but it is just as likely that they have finished early because they do not know the answers to many of the questions. So don't compare yourself to other students; it will only make you unnecessarily anxious and waste your time!

On your second go-through, first go back to those questions you've checked—the ones where you've narrowed down alternatives or have some idea of what the right answer might be. These are the questions that will be the easiest to answer, so you want to be sure to have time to do so. Then, if there's time, go back to those questions with a small dot—the ones that seem extremely difficult.

Here are some tips to help you decide on the best answer to questions about which you feel unsure. Your goal in this second go-through is to answer as many questions on the test as you can.

- *Read the directions for the section and the question again.* Make sure that your difficulty with the question is not due to misreading the directions or the question.
- *If the question seems particularly complicated, underline key words.* Sometimes emphasizing the key words will help to clarify the main idea of the question.
- *Put difficult questions into your own words.* Sometimes rephrasing a question can make it clear. But be careful not to inadvertently change the meaning.
- *If a question is not clear in spite of all your efforts to understand it, ask your instructor.* It is possible that a word might be missing or that there is a typographical error. (You can't ask the instructor for clarification of standardized tests, however, since the instructor must keep everything "standard" and cannot give special help to just one student.)
- *Reason through each question.* An acceptable alternative can be selected by a process of reasoning, knowledge, and elimination. For example, in multiple-choice or matching questions, balance the alternatives against each other; the differences may help you judge which is the best answer.
- *Try to recall your class lectures.* It is sometimes helpful to try to recall what your instructor said about the subject of a question that seems particularly difficult. Based on how your instructor presented the subject in class, try to figure out which answer he or she intended to be right.

- *Look for cues to help you answer the question.* Later in this chapter, you will learn about these cues, which include grammatical agreement, synonyms, qualifying and absolute words, position of alternatives, and inter-item cues.
- *Don't be afraid to change an answer* if, after going through the test the first time, you have reason to believe your first answer is wrong. Research shows that students who change their original answer choices because of careful reconsideration and discovering inter-item cues do increase their test scores. The key to successfully changing answers, however, is the ability to recognize the difference between a good reason to select a different answer and uncertainty about which is the right answer. Some students are better at recognizing this difference than others. To assess your ability to change answers for the better, save a few tests and compare the number of times you changed a wrong answer to a right one with the number of times you changed a right one to a wrong one.

Final Check

After having worked so hard to study for and take this test, you should be willing to spend the last five minutes before turning it in to make sure that there are no careless errors. Your final check should include the following steps.

1. *Go back to any answers you meant to change and make sure you made that change on the answer sheet.* Be sure to erase the original answer completely, especially if you have a machine-scorable answer sheet.
2. *Spot-check your answer sheet to be sure you put down the answers you intended.* If you left some answers blank the first time through, make sure that the following answers are where they belong—and weren't marked in the answer row you had left blank for the time being. If your answers were hastily written, fix the ones that might be misinterpreted by the person correcting the test.
3. *If there is no penalty for guessing, use the appropriate guessing strategy* at the end of this chapter to fill in any blanks on the answer sheet. *If there is a penalty for guessing, do not guess;* instead, try to find the question in the test. It is possible that you already worked out the answer but did not record it on the answer sheet.
4. *Quickly check for stray marks and erase them,* especially if you are using a machine-scorable answer sheet. Stray marks can be picked up by the test-scoring machine and counted as errors.
5. *Erase any dots, checks, and underlining on the test* (unless you were allowed to write your answers on the test). It is possible that other students will be using the same test, so you should turn it back in the same condition in which you received it. This is why your checks, dots, and underlining should be written in pencil, very lightly.

6. *Be sure your name and other necessary information is on every page of your test* (if your answers are marked on the test) *or answer sheet.* If you used scratch paper to work out problems or to jot down formulas or other information from memory, put your name on that, too, and label it "scratch sheet." Gather all these test materials and turn them in.

Test-Question Cues

Although it is no substitute for thorough study, knowing how to find cues to the answers in objective questions is an important skill for the testwise student. Some cues can be found in all (or several) kinds of objective tests: inter-item cues, grammatical agreement, singulars and plurals, word association and synonyms, and qualifying and absolute words. Other cues (length, position, and generality of multiple-choice alternatives, for example) are specific to a particular kind of objective test and will be explained in the following sections about each of the four kinds of objective questions.

Cues are more often found in teacher-made than in standardized tests. The publishers of standardized tests have huge staffs of test experts and spend a great deal of time and money to avoid flaws in their tests. Teachers, however, may not be experts in making test questions and do not have unlimited time or assistance to develop their tests. Consequently, most of the cues described in this chapter apply only to teacher-made tests.

A word of caution before you start to learn about these cues: do not spend a disproportionate amount of time searching for them. Use your knowledge of the course material to answer the questions; look for cues only if you are uncertain about the right answer.

Inter-Item Cues

One question in a test may provide information about the answer to another; this is an inter-item cue. It is difficult for an instructor to write a long objective exam covering a limited number of topics without having information in some questions that relates to other questions.

When you are not sure of the correct answer to a question, mark it to come back to the second time through. You might find information in another question that will give you the answer or at least help you eliminate one or more of the alternatives. As you work through a test, you may also find information that will give you a good reason to change a previous answer.

Inter-item cues are very important and very reliable. These are informational cues and can definitely help you get a better score. The other cues that will be discussed are probability cues, which can only increase your chances of answering a question correctly.

The following two questions are an example of an inter-item cue.

1. The orthograde skeletal structure of Homo sapiens is most similar to that of:
   A. beavers.
   B. apes.
   C. bears.
   D. deer.
37. An animal with an orthograde skeletal structure is said to:
   A. live in water.
   B. walk on two legs.
   C. walk on four legs.
   D. have no foramen magnum.

The first question tells you that Homo sapiens has an orthograde skeletal structure. Therefore, when you come to question 37, you can infer that B must be the correct answer. And, by selecting the correct answer to question 37, you could then infer that B was the correct answer to question 1 because the only one of the alternatives that walks on two legs is apes.

Inter-item cues can be used with matching questions to help you make matches you were uncertain of during the first go-through. They can also often tell you whether a statement is true or false. And they can often provide the answer to a completion question.

Qualifying and Absolute Words

An alternative or a statement that contains a qualifying word—such as *generally, often, some,* or *most*—is more likely to be correct than one that contains an absolute word—such as *always, never, all* or *nobody.* This is because there are very few things that are absolute, and it takes only one exception to make an absolute statement false or incorrect. For an example, compare the following two true-false questions.

1. All students know how to take tests.   True or False
2. Some students know how to take tests.   True or False

The word *all* in statement 1 makes it false because it is too inclusive. The word *some* in statement 2 makes it true; it acknowledges that there are some students who know how to take tests and some who do not.

In the boxes below there are absolute words that usually indicate a false statement or an incorrect alternative, and there are qualifying words that usually indicate a true statement or a correct alternative.

Absolute Words

always	everything	completely
never	everyone	exactly
necessarily	only	exclusively
definitely	no	cannot
must	without exception	no matter what
all	everybody	nobody
none	no one	
impossible	every	

Qualifying Words

generally	may	sometimes
usually	maybe	occasionally
some	most	often
frequently	on the average	perhaps
seldom	rarely	probably

Do not rely entirely on absolute and qualifying words to judge a statement or alternative, however. An experienced test-writer can make a false statement without using an absolute word. Or a theorem, law, or rule to which there is no exception at present can be presented with an absolute word and will be a true statement or correct alternative; for example, "E always equals mc²."

Sometimes there is not an absolute or a qualifying word in a statement or alternative, but it is stated in such a specific or absolute way that it is implied that there are no exceptions. These statements should be handled in the same way as statements with absolute words in them: Unless there can never be an exception, they should be considered false or incorrect. The following multiple-choice question provides an example.

1. When taking an objective test, it is a good idea to:
   A. never guess an answer.
   B. generally guess if you don't know the answer.
   C. cheat.
   D. usually expect to do very poorly.

Alternative C does not contain an absolute word, but *always* is implied. Therefore, you would reject C, just as you would reject A, which contains the absolute word *never*. That narrows your choices to B and D—and common sense (and having studied this book) would tell you that D is incorrect.

Grammatical Agreement

You can usually eliminate a choice if it does not grammatically agree with the stem of a multiple-choice or matching question or the sentence structure of a completion question. Sometimes the verb tenses or pronoun references do not agree. You may not be able to define the grammatical error, but you will know that somehow the choice does not sound right. Keep in mind, though, that typing errors can be made. If you feel fairly certain that an alternative is the right one even though it is not in grammatical agreement, pick it anyway.

Use of *A* and *An*.   The article *a* is used with words that begin with consonants, and the article *an* is used with words that begin with vowels. Although a careful test-writer would put an article with each alternative instead of in the stem, you might occasionally encounter a question such as the following one.

> 1. A biologist who specializes in the study of the relationships of an organism to its environment is known as an:
>   A. ecologist.
>   B. structuralist.
>   C. taxonomist.
>   D. naturalist.

Since the stem ends with the article *an*, the correct alternative must be A—ecologist—the only one that begins with a vowel.

Singular and Plural Verbs and Nouns.   Multiple-choice and completion questions both require you to complete a sentence. Your choice should make a grammatically correct sentence. So if the stem of a multiple-choice question uses a plural verb, the correct alternative will contain a plural noun or object; if the stem uses a singular verb, the alternative should also be singular. For example, if the alternatives to a stem that used *are* were (A) bone, (B) ear, (C) muscle, and (D) nerves, you would choose D, the only plural noun among the alternatives.

For a matching question, you can also use the singular-plural cue. A plural lead in Column 1 should match a plural alternative in Column 2, and a singular lead should match a singular alternative. For an example, look at the following matching question.

1. children	A. infants
2. female	B. boy and girl
3. male	C. woman
4. families	D. man
5. babies	E. mothers and their children

The only likely matches to 1, 4, and 5 are A, B, and E, since they are plural. Similarly, the only probable matches to 2 and 3 are C and D, the only singular choices. So even if you did not know the answers to this matching question, you could at least narrow down the choices by using the singular-plural cue.

Word Associations and Synonyms

In multiple-choice and matching questions, you may find that a word in the stem has a direct relationship to a word in one of the alternatives. The following multiple-choice question illustrates a synonym cue.

1. The *Strong Vocational Interest Blank* is used to measure:
    A. aptitudes.
    B. likes and dislikes.
    C. achievement.
    D. adjustment.

The word *interest* in the stem is synonymous with *likes and dislikes,* or alternative B. Of course, there will be questions in which the synonym is not the correct choice; if you recognize the correct answer, choose it rather than follow this cue.

Word-association cues are sometimes less obvious than synonyms, but you can find them by carefully reading the alternatives. The following multiple-choice question is an example of a word-association cue.

1. Charles Dickens' *Hard Times* is about the:
    A. difficult life of a factory worker.
    B. politics of the French chateau country.
    C. court of King Edward III.
    D. limitations of European existentialism.

Notice that the name of the book is *Hard Times*. The phrase "difficult life" in alternative A has about the same meaning. So even if you had not read the book, you could make an educated guess by using this cue.

Answering Multiple-Choice Questions

Your task is to read the stem, select the best possible alternative, and mark that answer on an answer sheet or the test itself. Selecting the best alternative is the hardest part of that task, but there are some techniques you can use to make it easier.

Anticipate the Answer

Multiple-choice tests often seem difficult because all the alternatives, or "foils," seem true. The instructions, however, usually tell the student to select the best alternative. That is why it is best to read the stem and then anticipate the answer before you read the alternatives. Once you have anticipated the answer, you can look for it among the alternatives offered.

Even though you may not anticipate the exact answer, it is probable that you will anticipate some major component of the answer. Therefore, as you read the alternatives, you can narrow the choices to those that contain that major component. One note of caution, however: Read and consider *all* the alternatives even if you first spot one that contains the major component you anticipated. It is possible that more than one alternative will contain the component, and you have to select the best one.

If the component you anticipated is not in any of the alternatives, focus on the choices offered and determine how well each of them answers the question. Select the one that makes the most sense in relation to the question.

Eliminate Unlikely Alternatives

The key to taking a multiple-choice test is the ability to eliminate answers, or narrow down the possibilities. This increases the odds that you will get the answer correct. Even if you are unsure of the material, by eliminating one or more of the alternatives, you increase your chances of selecting the correct alternative from those being offered.

To eliminate alternatives, you must apply your reasoning abilities. If you are asked to choose the correct theorem to be used for application to a geometry problem and you notice that one of the alternatives is not a theorem, then you would reason that the alternative should be eliminated.

When several alternatives seem correct, or if none of them do, you should compare them to see how they are alike or different. By balancing the alternatives against one another, you should be able to eliminate one or two based on what you know about the topic.

One way to eliminate alternatives is to treat each one as if it were a true-false statement. Lightly mark in pencil a T or an F by the alternative after you have read it with the stem.

Use Cues

In the preceding section, we have already looked at cues that are applicable to all or most kinds of objective questions: inter-item cues, qualifying and absolute words, grammatical agreement, and word association and synonyms. In addition, there are several cues that are specific to multiple-choice questions. These are cues that can be found in the alternatives.

The Most General Alternative. The correct alternative is often the most general, since the most general alternative often is the most encompassing of the choices. You will often find a list of items that have some very technical and specific alternatives and one that is more general. Chances are good that this is the correct answer. The following question is an example.

1. The lungs
   A. are solid and immobile and located within the chest.
   B. are the only organs that produce insulin.
   C. function primarily in respiration.
   D. possess the sphincter of Oddi.

Even if you aren't sure of the correct answer, you can see that the alternatives A, B, and D all deal with specific facts and details about the lungs. C deals with a main feature of the lungs—respiration. Since C is the more general answer and allows for more variability, it is logically the best one.

Two Similar Alternatives. If two alternatives have nearly the same meaning, then both are probably not correct—unless it is a key word or phrase that is different. For an example of a question that has two alternatives that mean essentially the same, read the following:

1. The Treaty of Brest Litovsk was ratified by Moscow because:
   A. Tsar Alexander I wanted to prevent Napoleon's invasion of Russia.
   B. Austria was outproducing Russia in armaments.
   C. Russia could not keep pace with the military production of its enemies.
   D. Lenin wanted to get the Soviet Union out of World War I.

Since alternatives B and C have very similar meanings, you should choose the answer from alternatives A or D. If two alternatives mean the same thing and only one correct answer is being asked for, you should eliminate the two similar answers.

Alternatives of Opposite Meaning. If two alternatives have the opposite meaning, one of them is probably the correct answer, because when the instructor is making alternatives for a question, an antonym for the correct answer is often the first thing that comes to mind. An example of a question with two alternatives of opposite meaning is the following:

1. The planarian has:
    A. an anterior brain.
    B. three legs.
    C. red eyes.
    D. a posterior brain.

The alternatives A and D are opposites. You can eliminate B and C, unless you know one of them is the correct answer. Since the alternatives A and D have opposite meanings, one of them is probably the correct answer.

None- or All-of-the-Above Alternatives. If one of the alternatives in a multiple-choice question is "none of the above" or "all of the above," the best approach is to read the stem and then, as you read each alternative, to decide if it is true or false. Lightly pencil a T or an F next to each alternative. When you come to the alternative that says "none of the above" or "all of the above," simply look back at what you decided about the alternatives above. If you indicated F by all of them, "none of the above" is probably the correct answer. And if you indicated T by all of them, the answer is probably "all of the above."

If you marked some T and some F, however, then eliminate "all of the above" or "none of the above" and pick your answer from the alternatives marked T. If you have four alternatives and one of them is "none of the above," two are marked F, and you are uncertain about the fourth one, your answer will either be "none of the above" or the fourth alternative.

A variation of the none- or all-of-the-above alternative is one indicating that two out of three (or three out of four) alternatives are correct; for example, "B and C above." If you marked B and C with a T, then that alternative is correct. If you marked one T and one F, then "B and C above" is not correct and should be eliminated.

The Middle Value. When the alternatives are numerical values or a range (from old to new, early to late, small to big, for example) and you are not sure which one is correct, you can usually eliminate the extremes. For an example, look at the following multiple-choice question.

1. The mature human has how many teeth?
    A. 15   B. 32   C. 54   D. 7

If you aren't sure of the answer, eliminate the two extreme values, C and D. Then choose one of the two middle values. (In this case, you could simply use the information available in your head—a count of your teeth would lead you to choose B!)

The Length of Alternatives. Many tests are fairly consistent about the length of correct answers. If you notice that most of the correct answers have been the shortest alternatives and you have no informational cues, pick the shortest of the possible alternatives. If most of the correct answers have been the longest, then pick the longest of the alternatives that have not been eliminated.

If you haven't noticed a tendency for the correct answers to be the longest or the shortest, the best chioce may be the longest alternative—if it is the most inclusive of the choices and does not contain or imply an absolute word.

The Position of Alternatives. Skim your answer sheet to see if most of the correct answers are in the same position. If there is a pattern and you have no other basis for selecting an alternative, then choose the answer in that position.

The alternative in the middle position, especially if it has the most words, is often the correct answer. Research has shown that in four-item multiple-choice questions, C is the answer slightly more often than the other alternatives. The position of alternatives is one of the weakest cues, however, since you don't know if your instructor has made a conscious effort to avoid the same position for the correct answers. This cue should be used only after you've searched for all other cues and if you have absolutely no idea of the correct answer.

Answering Matching Questions

Do not start answering a matching question until you have read the directions carefully. There may be more alternatives in Column 2 than there are stems in Column 1 and you will have alternatives left over. Or you may be asked to match more than one alternative with each stem. You may be directed to draw lines connecting the matches or you may have to write the letters identifying the alternatives beside their match in Column 1. If the directions are not clear, ask your instructor.

Read through both columns to get a sense of what all the choices are. Consider all the alternatives even if you first spot one that you think is a good match; it is possible that more than one alternative could fit.

To work through a matching question, you should follow these steps:
1. *On the first go-through, make all the matches you are sure of.* Check off the alternatives in Column 2 as you use them (unless the directions tell you that each alternative can be used more than once). The key to answering matching questions is the same as that to answering multiple-choice questions: Eliminate as many possibilities as you can.

2. *Leave the alternatives you are not sure of and work your way through the rest of the test.*
3. *Come back to the question when you discover an inter-item cue that will help you.*
4. *On your second go-through, come back to the unfinished matching questions and look for cues,* including those of grammatical agreement and word association discussed earlier in this chapter and the cues that are specific to matching questions, which we will look at now.

Matching-Question Cues

There are two special kinds of cues to look for in matching questions to help you narrow your choices: a mixture of categories and the position of the alternatives in Column 2.

Mixture of Categories.   In a matching question on a history test, for example, you might find names, dates, and events. In the first column, there may be stems of events and names to match with dates and events in the second column. Because it is not likely that you would match an event with an event and you would probably not match a date with a name, you can narrow your choices. The names in Column 1 should probably match events in Column 2 and the events in Column 1 should probably match dates in Column 2. Look at the example below and figure out the likely matches for the stems in Column 1.

Column 1	Column 2
1. Event	A. Date
2. Name	B. Event
3. Event	C. Date
4. Name	D. Event
5. Event	E. Date
6. Name	F. Event
7. Event	G. Date
8. Name	H. Event
9. Event	I. Date
10. Name	J. Event

Instead of having ten possible matches for each stem, you have only five. While five possible answers are still a lot, the probability of guessing correctly has increased—and your knowledge of the course material should help you narrow down that five even further. For stems 1, 3, 5, 7, and 9 in Column 1, you would select a match from alternatives A, C, E, G, and I in Column 2. For stems 2, 4, 6, 8, and 10, you would consider alternatives B, D, F, H, and J.

Position Cues. If you cannot decide between two or three matches, one cue that will increase the probability of selecting the best match is the position of the alternatives. It is likely that your instructor has tried not to put the matching alternative in Column 2 directly across from its stem in Column 1. So if one of the possible matches is across from the stem, you should probably assume that it is not the correct one.

Sometimes, the instructor will decide at the last minute to add one or two extra alternatives to Column 2 to make the question more challenging. Often these extras will be at the bottom of the column because the instructor doesn't have time to retype the entire question. Since you don't know whether your instructor was in a hurry to make the test, this is not a completely reliable cue. You should use it only after you have made all the matches you can based on your knowledge of the material and eliminated all the possible alternatives using the other kinds of cues. If you are left with an alternative in the middle of the list and one at the very bottom, go with the middle alternative.

The following matching question illustrates how to use position cues.

Directions: Write the letter of the correct answer from Column 2 in the answer blank next to Column 1. Use each answer only once.

Answers	Column 1	Column 2
_C_	1. anthropologist	√A. community and family life
_d_	2. astronomer	√B. meanings and psychological effects of words
_____	3. geologist	
_g_	4. biologist	√C. human development
_g_	5. botanist	√D. celestial phenomena
_d_	6. zoologist	E. language
_____	7. entomologist	F. insect forms
_____	8. philologist	G. the earth
_B_	9. semanticist	√H. all forms of living matter
_a_	10. sociologist	√I. animal life
		√J. plant life
		K. problems of aging
		L. mental disease

You have used your knowledge and other cues to make the matches shown in the answer column, and you have checked off the alternatives in Column 2 that you have matched. But you have no idea of the answers to stems 3, 7, and 8, and you have five alternatives left in Column 2. By using the same-line position cue, you can probably eliminate G as a match for 7.

By using the end-of-the-column position cue, you can probably eliminate K and L entirely. Therefore, the answer to 7 is most likely E or F. If you picked F (which is the correct match), you would be left with alternatives E and G to match with stems 3 and 8. You can use your knowledge and reasoning ability to choose, or, if that isn't any help, you can simply guess (and you would have a 50-50 chance of being correct). If you guessed correctly, you would have put G next to 3 and E next to 8.

Answering True-False Questions

True-false questions test not only your knowledge of the material but also your ability to do careful and critical reading. You must pay attention to every word in a true-false statement, but you must guard against reading information into it that isn't there and against trying too hard to find exceptions to every statement. To illustrate the problem with overinterpreting, read the following statement.

> 1. Psychology is the science that studies why human beings behave as they do. True or False?

You might be tempted to say that this statement is false because you remember from your notes that psychology also studies animal behavior. The testwise student realizes, however, that just because this statement does not contain an exhaustive definition of psychology, it should not be judged false. If the statement had been worded "Psychology studies only human behavior," however, then you would have marked it false; the *only* incorrectly limits the statement.

The hardest kind of true-false question is the mixed statement; in other words, one part is true and the other part is false. You need to remember that unless the entire statement is true, you should mark it false. A true-false test can also be made more challenging by asking you to underline the elements that make statements false or to revise false statements to make them true ones. Be sure to read the test directions carefully.

When answering a series of true-false questions, don't get bogged down on any one of them. Keep up your speed, allotting only the length of time you scheduled for each question in the first go-through. Leave the questions that you're not sure of until the second go-through. As you continue through the test, look for inter-item cues. When you come back to the questions you couldn't answer, use the cues of qualifying and absolute words discussed earlier in this chapter as well.

Unlike multiple-choice tests, the pattern of answers is irrelevant in true-false tests. It does not matter if you have a long series of trues or of falses or if you have many more trues than falses or vice versa. The pattern of answers is not a cue in true-false tests.

Answering Completion Questions

Completion, or fill-in-the-blank, questions are the most difficult kind of objective questions because you must recall the right answer rather than recognize it among a number of alternatives. As with the other kinds of objective questions, however, it is important to read the directions and the questions very carefully.

Some of the cues that apply to the other objective questions will be useful in helping you answer completion questions, too. Look for cues of grammatical agreement. Is the word before the blank *a* or *an*? That can tell you whether the missing word starts with a vowel or a consonant. Are the verbs, nouns, or pronouns that refer to the missing word singular or plural?

When you think of an answer to fill in, read the completed sentence quietly to yourself. Does it sound right? Sometimes hearing the sentence will help you decide if you've made the right choice and stimulate your memory.

Of course, inter-item cues are the most helpful. As with the other kinds of objective tests, skip the questions you're not sure of the first time through. After going through the rest of the test, you may discover the answer in another question.

The length of the line to be filled in can sometimes be a cue—but it is not very reliable. Someone besides your instructor may have typed the test and not have known what the intended answers were. Or your instructor might have made all the blanks uniform to avoid this kind of cue or simply have made blanks that fit the available space.

Be aware that the answer may be more than one word; it could be a phrase or a sentence. If the directions do not tell you, you should ask the instructor before you start the test.

Sometimes you may not be sure that you have recalled the exact word the instructor is looking for. If that is the case, go ahead and write down the word or phrase that comes to mind because the instructor might give you partial credit for having the general idea.

When and How to Guess

When you've come to the limits of your knowledge and you've just about run out of time, your last resort—for some tests—is to guess. But first, you need to know whether there will be a penalty for guessing; if this is not indicated in the test directions, ask your instructor before you even start to take the test (asking in the last three minutes of the test would be a dead giveaway!)

On most teacher-made tests, departmental tests, and many standardized tests, there is no penalty for guessing. This means that your score will be based only on the number of correct answers; incorrect answers will not be subtracted from your score. In this case, you would want to answer every item on the test whether you knew the answer or not.

On some standardized tests, there is a penalty for guessing. This usually means that one point (or however many points the question is worth) is subtracted for each unanswered question, but a fraction more than the value of the question is subtracted for each incorrect answer. The purpose of this penalty is to discourage students from wild guessing.

The amount of the penalty should determine how much to guess. If the penalty is only one-fourth more than the value of the question, for example, and you can eliminate (by your knowledge or by cues in the test) at least one of the alternatives, you should go ahead and guess. If the penalty is greater—say, one-and-a-half times the value of the question—you should guess only if you have narrowed the possible alternatives to two.

If your time is almost up and you have not answered 15 or 20 percent of the questions on the test (which can easily happen on a standardized or very long test), you should use the last minute to do some wild guessing and answer every question if there is no penalty for guessing. Since you might not want the person scoring the test to know that you were guessing, you shouldn't put all your wild guesses in the same column; rather, mark a random variety of answer positions.

Try the guessing experiments that follow to see how many points you could pick up by randomly guessing on a true-false test and on a four-alternative multiple-choice test. Compare your random answers to those in the back of the book. Give yourself two points for each question you answered correctly; if you answer all of them correctly, your score would be 100 points for each test.

Exercise 8.1
Experimental True-False Test

Directions: Put a T or an F beside each number. Compare your answers with those at the back of the book. Each "correct" response counts two points. Your score is based on the numbr of correct answers.

1. _____	11. _____	21. _____	31. _____	41. _____
2. _____	12. _____	22. _____	32. _____	42. _____
3. _____	13. _____	23. _____	33. _____	43. _____
4. _____	14. _____	24. _____	34. _____	44. _____
5. _____	15. _____	25. _____	35. _____	45. _____
6. _____	16. _____	26. _____	36. _____	46. _____
7. _____	17. _____	27. _____	37. _____	47. _____
8. _____	18. _____	28. _____	38. _____	48. _____
9. _____	19. _____	29. _____	39. _____	49. _____
10. _____	20. _____	30. _____	40. _____	50. _____

Your Wild Guessing Score _____

Exercise 8.2
Experimental Multiple-Choice Test

Directions: Put A, B, C, or D beside each number. Compare your answers with those at the back of the book. Each "correct" response counts two points. Your score is based on the number of correct answers.

1. _____	11. _____	21. _____	31. _____	41. _____
2. _____	12. _____	22. _____	32. _____	42. _____
3. _____	13. _____	23. _____	33. _____	43. _____
4. _____	14. _____	24. _____	34. _____	44. _____
5. _____	15. _____	25. _____	35. _____	45. _____
6. _____	16. _____	26. _____	36. _____	46. _____
7. _____	17. _____	27. _____	37. _____	47. _____
8. _____	18. _____	28. _____	38. _____	48. _____
9. _____	19. _____	29. _____	39. _____	49. _____
10. _____	20. _____	30. _____	40. _____	50. _____

Your Wild Guessing Score _____

The purpose of these two experiments is not to show you that there's some chance you could pass an objective test without studying; to be sure of a good score, there is no substitute for studying. The purpose is to show you that on tests where there is no penalty for guessing, you could probably add a few points to your score by randomly answering the questions that you did not have time to finish.

Many students feel timid about guessing. They may know that they can increase their score by guessing but refuse to do so because they believe it is unfair or dishonest to guess. But some standardized tests and many departmental and teacher-made tests are graded on a curve. This means that the highest scorers will get the A's or get admitted to a college or a special program, while the lower scorers will get the lower grades and will not be admitted. If you knew just as much about the subject of a test as several other members of your class, but they were willing to guess as a last resort and you were not, they would get higher scores than you would.

There is another benefit to being willing to guess, too. When you do not answer a question, you signal the instructor that you know nothing about that question. But the chances are that you do have some idea about it and have perhaps even narrowed the alternatives. By guessing one of the remaining alternatives you have a chance to get credit for what you know.

In summary, the best guarantee to getting a good grade is thorough study. But you can add some points to your score by guessing at the answer after you have eliminated obviously wrong alternatives, and you can add a few more by wild guessing (if there is no penalty for guessing) if time runs out before you have gone through all the questions.

Chapter Summary

Just as there are strategy and techniques for studying for a test, there are strategy and techniques for taking a test. For an objective test, it is important to budget your time so you will be able to answer all the questions. And the best way to answer all the questions is to do the easy ones the first time through the test, come back to the difficult ones the second time through and use cues to help decide on the answer, and then to go through it one more time for a final check for careless errors.

Testwise students know how to look for inter-item cues, which are reliable, informational cues, and for the probability cues of grammatical agreement, qualifying and absolute words, and word associations and synonyms. They also know about the cues that are specific to multiple-choice and matching questions.

Above all, they know the importance of reading the directions and the questions carefully and of being willing to guess, if there is no penalty for guessing, as a last resort.

A Final Word

By now you have discovered that testwiseness is really just good preparation and effective test-taking, combined with knowing the right cues to use when knowledge is incomplete. The more you use these organization, preparation, and test-taking strategies, the better you will become at taking tests or being testwise.

It is just not enough to really know your subject, although that certainly is a major factor. You must also know how to take different kinds of tests. Tests that will sample your knowledge of the subject, as well as measure your ability to take tests. Being testwise is not a trick; it is having essential study skills—skills that make sense and are used by the most prepared, knowledgeable, and successful students.

A TestWise Test

Now that you have finished working through the chapters, you should be on your way to becoming testwise. All it will take is practice—and you'll have plenty of opportunities to do that!

To give yourself a chance to see how testwise you are and whether there are any points you should review, here's one final exercise. You can set your own time for taking this test (you can even use it to practice making a test-taking schedule, if you like). Each answer is worth 1 point (note that many questions have more than one answer; each match and each item in a list count as one answer, for example). There is a possible total of 100 points with no penalty for guessing. After you've finished, compare your answers with those at the back of the book and count up your points.

Part One: Getting Started

Chapter 1: Avoiding Test Panic

1. Anxiety about tests
    A. can be desirable.
    B. is normal.
    C. can be excessive.
    D. all of the above.
    E. none of the above.

    Answer: _____

2. To psych yourself up for a test, you need to think about how it relates to your _____ .

3. Which of the following should you not do when preparing for a test?
    A. Allow yourself some quiet leisure time.
    B. Get a normal amount of sleep every night.
    C. Avoid physical activity.
    D. Reward yourself for hard work.
    E. All of the above.

    Answer: _____

4. It is advisable to stay up all night just before a test, but not to finish a paper.

    True _____ or False _____ ? If false, underline the word or words that make it so.

5. Describe three relaxation techniques.

    (1) _____

    _____

    _____

    (2) _____

    _____

    _____

    (3) _____

    _____

    _____

6. To build a thorough set of lecture notes, you should never
    A. use abbreviations and symbols.
    B. copy someone's notes if you've been absent.
    C. fill in gaps in your notes the same day of the class.
    D. record your instructor's examples exactly.
    E. none of the above.

    Answer: _____

7. To read a textbook chapter step-by-step, you should (1) look at the pictures,

    tables, and charts; (2) read the _____ ; (3) read the bold print;

    (4) read the _____ ; (5) read the questions or discussion points;

    (6) _____ ; (7) read the chapter text; and, if there's time,

    (8) _____ .

Chapter 2: Developing a Game Plan

8. On a master test schedule, you should indicate:
    A. dates of tests.
    B. contents of tests.
    C. course names.
    D. midterms and finals.
    E. all of the above.

    Answer: _____

9. A test analysis form helps you predict the format, time, and content of a test.

    True _____ or False _____ ? If false, underline the word or words that make it so.

10. You should use old tests to identify your general strengths and weaknesses and to memorize the answers.

    True _____ or False _____ ? If false, underline the word or words that make it so.

11. What three questions do you need to answer to plan a study schedule for a test?

    (1) _____

    (2) _____

    (3) _____

12. To plan your study schedule for a test, you need to:
    A. find time to finish all readings and assignments.
    B. set priorities.
    C. assign every free hour to study.
    D. all of the above.
    E. none of the above.

    Answer: _____

13. The most important thing to do the day and night before an exam is to

    _____ and _____ the material.

14. To study for midterms and finals, you should allow yourself:
    A. the entire term.
    B. two to three weeks.
    C. one to two weeks.
    D. four days.
    E. one week.

    Answer: _____

15. Your game plan for studying for a test should include:
    A. a master test schedule.
    B. a test analysis form.
    C. a study schedule for two weeks.
    D. daily lists of things to do.
    E. all of the above.

    Answer: _____

Part Two: Preparing for Tests

Chapter 3: Test-Study Techniques

16. An essay test requires recognition memory.

    True _____ or False _____ ? If false, underline the word or words that make it so.

17. List three resources from which to make study notes, in addition to your test analysis form.

    (1) _____

    (2) _____

    (3) _____

18. It is best to recite and memorize your
   A. readings.
   B. class notes.
   C. test analysis form.
   D. condensed study notes.
   E. none of the above.

   Answer: _____

19. Match the memorization technique with the kind of information to be memorized. Some techniques apply to more than one kind of information.

   _____ 1. Association
   _____ 2. Mnemonic connection
   _____ 3. Whole learning

   A. Poem
   B. Word definitions
   C. Speech
   D. Words in a specific order
   E. Multi-word title

20. Because physical activity helps to promote recall, you should

   _____ and _____ information to be memorized.

21. Cramming is rote repetition, review, and reciting done just before a test.

   True _____ or False _____ ? If false, underline the word or words that make it so.

Chapter 4: Preparing for Essay Tests

22. Predicting essay questions helps you:
   A. actively think about the material.
   B. decide what information to memorize.
   C. practice essay answers.
   D. all of the above.
   E. none of the above.

   Answer: _____

23. Match the kind of notes to the kind of essay question that is likely to be asked from them.

   _____ 1. A list of people or things
   _____ 2. Steps of a process or historical development
   _____ 3. Two or more things
   _____ 4. Specific individual, situation, or institution

   A. Long-answer trace question
   B. Long-answer discussion question
   C. Long-answer compare-and-contrast question
   D. Short-answer question

24. To research some topics, you can refer to:
    A. the *Current Biography Index.*
    B. *The Readers' Guide to Periodical Literature.*
    C. the current *Statistical Abstract of the United States.*
    D. B and C above.
    E. all of the above.

    Answer: _____

25. When practicing answers for your essay questions, you should start off by turning the questions into statements.

    True _____ or False _____ ? If false, underline the word or words that make it so.

Chapter 5: Preparing for Objective Tests

26. An objective test requires recognition memory.

    True _____ or False _____ ? If false, underline the word or words that make it so.

27. Match the descriptions with the type of objective questions.

    _____ 1. Multiple-choice   A. A statement with a blank

    _____ 2. Matching   B. A stem and three to five alternatives

    _____ 3. True-false   C. Two columns

    _____ 4. Completion   D. A statement

28. Students who prepare for objective tests as thoroughly as they do for essay tests usually score higher than do students who have prepared only enough to recognize the right answers.

    True _____ or False _____ ? Why? _____

    _____

Part Three: Taking Tests
Chapter 6: Getting Organized to Take the Test

29. You should try to arrive at the test room about 15 minutes early. List three things you should do during that time.

    (1) _____

    (2) _____

    (3) _____

30. There are several things to do before you start answering questions on a test. One of them is to jot down memorized facts.

   True _____ or False _____ ? Why? _____

   _____

31. It is also very important to listen to all directions that your instructor gives.

   True _____ or False _____ ? Why? _____

   _____

32. If you are right-handed, put the exam on the right side of the desk and the answer sheet on the left.

   True _____ or False _____ ? If false, underline the word or words that make it so.

Chapter 7: Taking an Essay Test

33. You should always spend the same amount of time on every essay test question no matter how many points it is worth.

   True _____ or False _____ ? If false, underline the word or words that make it so.

34. List the four tasks to allot time for in your essay test schedule.

   (1) _____

   (2) _____

   (3) _____

   (4) _____

35. To give logical order to your essay, you should _____ it first.

36. The opening statement of an essay answer should _____ the question.

37. A deductive pattern in an essay means going from the main idea to the details.

   True _____ or False _____ ? If false, underline the word or words that make it so.

38. You should always try to provide specific dates and numbers in your essay answers.

   True _____ or False _____ ? If false, underline the word or words that make it so.

Chapter 8: Taking an Objective Test

39. Match the appropriate amount of time with each step of taking an objective test that is 55 minutes long and has 50 equally weighted questions.

    _____ 1. Read directions and plan schedule   A. 5 minutes

    _____ 2. First go-through   B. 20 minutes

    _____ 3. Second go-through   C. 25 minutes

    _____ 4. Final check

40. On your first go-through, you should:
    A. answer only the easier questions.
    B. answer every question.
    C. mark questions you're unsure of.
    D. A and C.
    E. None of the above.

    Answer: _____

41. List three ways to try to figure out difficult questions on your second go-through.

    (1) _____

    (2) _____

    (3) _____

42. Match the types of questions in Column 2 to the appropriate test-question cues in Column 1. Some questions can be matched to more than one cue. (Hint: there are a total of 11 possible matches.)

    _____ 1. Inter-item cue   A. Multiple-choice

    _____ 2. Qualifying and absolute words   B. Matching

    _____ 3. Grammatical agreement   C. True-false

    _____ 4. Synonyms   D. Completion

43. A good strategy for answering multiple-choice questions is to try to:
    A. anticipate the answer.
    B. eliminate alternatives.
    C. use cues.
    D. all of the above.
    E. none of the above.

    Answer: _____

44. If you don't know an answer, you should always guess.

   True _____ or False _____ ?   Why? _____

   _____

45. If there is no penalty for guessing, you should always answer each question, even if you have to guess.

   True _____ or False _____ ?   Why? _____

   _____

Answers to Exercises

The answers here are only for those exercises for which the right answers can be expressed in only one way. Because the answers will vary for practice essays, there are no answers for Exercises 4.5, 4.6, or 4.7 here. You might ask an instructor or a friend to evaluate them, or you might come back to them a day or two after writing them and evaluate them yourself.

Exercise 2.1 (pages 19–20)

1. 9/26
2. English
3. Vocabulary
4. no
5. English, Math, Psychology
6. (a) English and Math
   (b) Math, because it is a big midterm test and the English test is only a weekly vocabulary test.
7. English, Biology
8. Vocabulary or English; no
9. Week 2: Math, Chapters 1–3
   Week 3: Psychology, Unit 1
   Week 4: Math, Chapters 4–6
   Week 7: Math, Chapters 7–9
   Week 8: Psychology, Unit 3
   Week 9: Math, Chapters 10–12
   Although these tests are not as big as a midterm or final, all of them are bigger than a weekly vocabulary test and would probably be a larger percentage of the grade than a weekly test.

10. (a) Biology, Math, English, Psychology
    (b) English and Psychology
    (c) Biology and Math

Exercise 2.2 (page 27)

1. textbook, class notes
2. no
3. (a) What is psychology and how is it different from psychiatry? History of psychology and four schools of psychology.
   (b) Each of these two areas will count 30 percent, while each of the other two will only count 20 percent.
   (c) Long-answer essays
   (d) Yes, because these two areas make up 60 percent of the test and the other areas make up only 40 percent of the test.
4. Yes
   Definitions of major fields of psychology, definitions of the methods of psychology, the four schools of psychology, names and relative time periods from the history of psychology
5. Yes

Exercise 3.1 (pages 47–49)

Psych Notes

3   Abnormal Psych.—studies all forms of abnormal human behavior.

3   Clinical Psych.—deals with normal and abnormal behavior, and with indiv. psychol. adjustment to oneself and one's environment.

3   Comparative Psych.—studies behavior and abilities of different animal species.

3   Developmental Psych.—studies changes in human behavior from birth to old age.

3   Educational Psych.—applies the principles of psych. to the ed. process.

/   Psychology is the science that studies why human beings and animals behave as they do. The psychologist is interested in understanding the whole range of human experience.

/   Psychology is one of the behavioral sciences, like biology, sociology, and anthropology.

/   Psychiatry is a medical science dealing mostly with mental illness. Psychology studies all kinds of behavior, normal as well as abnormal. Psychiatrists are physicians with M.D. degrees and special training in the field of mental illness. Most psychologists have a Ph.D. or M.A. degree instead of medical school training.

4   1. Experiments—the experimental method enables a psychologist to control the conditions that determine the aspect of behavior being studied.

4   2. Natural Observations—the direct observation of human behavior in its natural environment.

4   3. Case Histories—collection of info. about an individual's past and present life.

4   4. Surveys—the psychol. interviews members of a group by written questionnaires or orally. The psychol. can pull the info. together and draw conclusions about average attitudes or behavior.

N/A   Psychological problems are often categorized by the terms: 1. neurosis, 2. psychosis, 3. paranoia, 4. schizophrenia, and 5. depression.

2   Behaviorism—Watson—1913—reaction against structuralism. Watson called for the study of the observable behavior of humans and animals—not of their experiences.

2   Gestalt Psychology—concerned with the organization of mental processes—we perceive organized patterns and the whole—Wertheimer, Kohler, Koffka, Lewin.

2   Psychoanalysis—Freud—early 1900s—developed a theory to explain why people become emotionally disturbed—people repress the needs and desires that are unacceptable to themselves or society.

N/A   Careers in Psychology—for info. write Amer. Psych. Assoc., 1200 17th St., N.W., Washington, D.C. 20036.

3   Industrial Psych.—applies psych. principles and techniques to the needs and problems of industry.

3   Physiological Psych.—concerned with relationship between behavior and the function of the nervous system.

3   Social Psych.—studies relationships among people in groups and the formation of public opinion.

3   Personality studies—studies the diff. characteristics of people and how these characteristics develop and can be measured.

3   Perception studies—studies the process by which patterns of environmental energies become known as objects, events, people, and other aspects of the world.

2   Structuralism—Wundt—thought main purpose of psych. was to describe and analyze conscious experience, including sensations, images, and feelings of which only the person himself is aware.

Exercise 4.1 (pages 59–60)
(wording may vary slightly)
1. Name the main characters in *Gone with the Wind* and identify their traits.
2. Identify three late-19th-century American authors and list their works.

Exercise 4.2 (pages 61–62)
(wording may vary slightly)
1. Trace the distribution of product from the manufacturer.
2. Trace the events leading to the Great Depression.

Exercise 4.3 (pages 64–65)
(wording may vary slightly)

1. Compare and contrast the three main characters in Ken Kesey's *One Flew Over the Cuckoo's Nest.*
2. Compare and contrast the great American art forms and works of Georgia O'Keeffe, Louis Tiffany, and Frank Lloyd Wright.

Exercise 4.4 (pages 67–68)
(wording may vary slightly)

1. Discuss the effects of the bombings of Hiroshima and Nagasaki.
2. Discuss the significance of the Jim Crow laws in the segregationist and the civil rights movements.

Exercise 7.1 (pages 97–98)

1. contrast
2. analyze, criticize, evaluate, or review
3. describe or trace
4. give an example or illustrate
5. summarize or relate
6. describe or outline
7. analyze, discuss, or review
8. enumerate, list, name, describe, or outline
9. define or explain
10. compare, relate, or analyze

Exercise 7.2 (pages 100–101)
(wording may vary slightly)

1. *Exam Term(s):* identify. *Subject:* three late-nineteenth-century American authors and their works. *Opening Statement:* Three late-nineteenth-century American authors were Samuel Clemens (or Mark Twain), Edith Wharton, and Henry James.
2. *Exam Term(s):* describe. *Subject:* steps in formation of RNA. *Opening Statement:* RNA is formed by the following steps:
3. *Exam Term(s):* trace. *Subject:* events leading to Revolutionary War in America. *Opening Statement:* The following important events led to the Revolutionary War in America.
4. *Exam Term(s):* compare and contrast. *Subject:* art forms and works of Georgia O'Keeffe, Louis Tiffany, and Frank Lloyd Wright. *Opening Statement:* The great American art forms and works of Georgia O'Keeffe, Louis Tiffany, and Frank Lloyd Wright include:
5. *Exam Term(s):* discuss. *Subject:* effects of Civil War in America. *Opening Statement:* Some of the effects of the Civil War in America were the following:

Exercise 8.1 (page 124)

1. T	11. T	21. T	31. T	41. T
2. T	12. T	22. T	32. T	42. T
3. F	13. T	23. T	33. T	43. F
4. T	14. T	24. T	34. F	44. F
5. F	15. F	25. T	35. F	45. F
6. F	16. T	26. F	36. T	46. T
7. T	17. T	27. T	37. F	47. T
8. F	18. F	28. F	38. F	48. T
9. F	19. T	29. F	39. F	49. T
10. F	20. F	30. F	40. T	50. F

Exercise 8.2 (page 124)

1. B	11. C	21. B	31. C	41. B
2. C	12. C	22. D	32. C	42. B
3. C	13. D	23. C	33. C	43. C
4. A	14. B	24. D	34. B	44. D
5. B	15. C	25. B	35. D	45. C
6. C	16. C	26. A	36. B	46. C
7. D	17. B	27. C	37. A	47. A
8. D	18. A	28. C	38. C	48. B
9. A	19. B	29. D	39. C	49. D
10. B	20. C	30. A	40. D	50. C

A TestWise Test (pages 127–135)

The number of points is 100. As you compare your answers with the ones below, note your score for each question in the blank beside the point value. (Note that each part of your answer is worth 1 point.) Then, add up your scores at the end to see how testwise you've become. If you miss questions, go back and reread the appropriate chapter parts.

_____ (1 pt.)   1. D

_____ (1 pt.)   2. ultimate goal in life

_____ (1 pt.)   3. C

_____ (2 pts.)   4. False
all night

_____ (3 pts.)   5. (three of the following four)
(1) Inhale deeply with your eyes closed, hold your breath, and then exhale slowly.
(2) Sit back in your chair, loosen your entire body, and close your eyes for a few minutes.
(3) Tighten all your muscles, hold them, and then let them all loosen.
(4) Tighten your muscles and then systematically loosen each one, one at a time.

_____ (1 pt.)   6. E

_____ (4 pts.)   7. (2) introduction
                      (4) summary
                      (6) skim
                      (8) take notes

_____ (1 pt.)   8. E

_____ (2 pts.)   9. True
                      Since the statement is true, no words should be underlined.

_____ (2 pts.) 10. False
                      <u>and to memorize the answers</u>

_____ (3 pts.) 11. (1) How much time is available to study?
                      (2) How good a grade do I need?
                      (3) How much time will I need to study?

_____ (1 pt.)   12. B

_____ (2 pts.) 13. review, recite

_____ (1 pt.)   14. B

_____ (1 pt.)   15. E

_____ (2 pts.) 16. False
                      <u>recognition</u>

_____ (3 pts.) 17. (three of any of the following)
                      class notes, textbooks, library materials, handouts, lab notes, assignments

_____ (1 pt.)   18. D

_____ (5 pts.) 19. (1) B
                      (2) D, E
                      (3) A, C

_____ (2 pts.) 20. recite, write

_____ (2 pts.) 21. True
                      Since the statement is true, no words should be underlined.

_____ (1 pt.)   22. D

_____ (4 pts.) 23. (1) D
                      (2) A
                      (3) C
                      (4) B

_____ (1 pt.)   24. D

_____ (2 pts.) 25. True
                      Since the statement is true, no words should be underlined.

_____ (2 pts.)   26. True

Since the statement is true, no words should be underlined.

_____ (4 pts.)   27. (1) B

(2) C

(3) D

(4) A

_____ (2 pts.)   28. True

Because they have a more thorough knowledge of the material.

_____ (3 pts.)   29. (three of the following four)

(1) review and recite memorized notes

(2) find a comfortable seat

(3) organize your materials

(4) practice relaxation techniques

_____ (2 pts.)   30. True

You will not risk forgetting these facts while you look over questions and begin to answer them.

_____ (2 pts.)   31. True

It is important to understand all directions before starting the test.

_____ (2 pts.)   32. False

right side of the desk and the answer sheet on the left

_____ (2 pts.)   33. False

always and/or no matter how many points it is worth

_____ (4 pts.)   34. (1) assessment and scheduling

(2) answering questions

(3) rereading and finishing answers

(4) final checking

_____ (1 pt.)   35. outline

_____ (1 pt.)   36. rephrase

_____ (1 pt.)   37. True

Since the statement is true, no words should be underlined.

_____ (1 pt.)   38. False

always and/or specific dates and numbers

_____ (4 pts.)   39. (1) A

(2) C

(3) B

(4) A

_____ (1 pt.)   40. D

_____ (3 pts.)   41. (three of the following six)
                    (1) Reread the directions and question.
                    (2) Underline key words in question.
                    (3) Ask the instructor to clarify question.
                    (4) Reason through the question.
                    (5) Try to recall class lectures.
                    (6) Look for cues.

_____ (11 pts.)   42. (1) A, B, C, D
                    (2) A, C
                    (3) A, B, D
                    (4) A, B

_____ (1 pt.)   43. D

_____ (2 pts.)   44. False
                    There may be a penalty for guessing.

_____ (2 pts.)   45. True
                    You have nothing to lose by guessing, if there is no penalty. If you don't answer questions you signal to the instructor that you know nothing about those questions, but if you can narrow the alternatives and then guess a few answers correctly, you will get some credit.

_____ Your Total TestWise Score

Appendix

Master Test Schedule for Term

Test Dates & Content	Course Names					
Week 1						
Week 2						
Week 3						
Week 4						
Week 5						
Week 6						
Week 7						
Week 8						
Week 9						
Week 10						
Week 11						
Week 12						
Week 13						
Week 14						
Week 15						
Week 16						
Finals Week						

Test Analysis for Individual Tests

Class _____   Instructor _____

Date of Test _____   Time of Day _____

% of Grade _____   Major or Minor Test _____

What is the *format* of the test?

Essay: _____ Long-Answer (discuss, trace, compare and contrast)

_____ Short-Answer (list, name, define, identify)

Objective: _____ True-False

_____ Multiple-Choice

_____ Matching

_____ Completion (fill-in-the-blank)

How many questions will be on the test? _____

How many of each kind of question will be on it?

_____ Long-Answer Essay   _____ True-False

_____ Short-Answer Essay   _____ Multiple-Choice

_____ Matching

_____ Completion

How much time will I have for the test? _____

What is the *content* of the test? _____

Topics or Kinds of Problems	Sources of Content (notes, readings, labs)	% of Score and # of Questions	Format of Questions*
_____	_____	_____	_____
_____	_____	_____	_____
_____	_____	_____	_____
_____	_____	_____	_____
_____	_____	_____	_____
_____	_____	_____	_____

Are details or general concepts important? _____

Do I have to know formulas or theorems? _____ If so, which ones?* _____

_____

Do I have to know definitions? _____ If so, which ones?* _____

_____

Do I have to know important names and dates? _____ If so, which ones?* _____

_____

_____

_____

Will points be taken off for spelling errors? _____

Can I bring a dictionary to use during the test? _____

Can I bring a calculator to use during the test? _____

If problems have to be worked out, how much credit is given for accuracy? _____ and how

much for method? _____

Will this be an open-book test? _____

Are copies of previous exams available for inspection? _____

Is this a departmental test or one made up by the instructor? _____

Who will grade this test?** _____

Do the writer and grader of this test have any special biases?** _____

_____

Additional Clues or Notes:**

_____

_____

_____

Notes: * You may not be able to find this out before the test.
        ** You shouldn't ask this question of the instructor.

Schedule: Two Weeks Before _____ Test

Hour	Mon.	Tues.	Wed.	Thurs.	Fri.	Sat.	Sun.
A.M.							
12–1							
1–2							
2–3							
3–4							
4–5							
5–6							
6–7							
7–8							
8–9							
9–10							
10–11							
11–12							
P.M.							
12–1							
1–2							
2–3							
3–4							
4–5							
5–6							
6–7							
7–8							
8–9							
9–10							
10–11							
11–12							

Schedule: Week Before _____ Test

Hour	Mon.	Tues.	Wed.	Thurs.	Fri.	Sat.	Sun.
A.M.							
12–1							
1–2							
2–3							
3–4							
4–5							
5–6							
6–7							
7–8							
8–9							
9–10							
10–11							
11–12							
P.M.							
12–1							
1–2							
2–3							
3–4							
4–5							
5–6							
6–7							
7–8							
8–9							
9–10							
10–11							
11–12							

Schedule: Week of _____ Test

Hour	Mon.	Tues.	Wed.	Thurs.	Fri.	Sat.	Sun.
A.M.							
12–1							
1–2							
2–3							
3–4							
4–5							
5–6							
6–7							
7–8							
8–9							
9–10							
10–11							
11–12							
P.M.							
12–1							
1–2							
2–3							
3–4							
4–5							
5–6							
6–7							
7–8							
8–9							
9–10							
10–11							
11–12							

Things-to-Do-List

Things to Do to

Study for _____ Test   Day or Date   Time

Game Plan Checklist

To make sure that your game plan for studying for each test is complete, check off the items in this list as you get them done.

_____ 1. Did I prepare a *master test schedule* for the term, putting in all my test dates?

_____ 2. Did I cross out all my fixed commitments on the *schedules for one week before the test and the week of the test* (two weeks before midterm and final tests) and note when I have other tests during those weeks?

_____ 3. Did I figure out when I have *study time available* on these schedules for each test?

_____ 4. Did I prepare a *test analysis form* using information from class, from the instructor, and from other sources?

_____ 5. Have I checked to see if there are *past exams* available for review?

_____ 6. Using my test analysis form and past exams (if they were available), did I determine *the format of the test* so I know whether to prepare for objective or essay questions?

_____ 7. Using my test analysis form, did I assess *where I am right now in terms of readings* and other assignments related to the test?

_____ 8. Did I make a complete *list of things to do* to prepare for the test, putting the most important items first and planning when to do them according to the time available on my study schedule?

_____ 9. Am I going to break down the things-to-do list into *daily lists* on cards?

Once you have checked off all the items on this list, you are ready for the next step: preparing and studying for your test!